OTHER TITLES BY C.L. BROWN

Loud Whispers of Silent Souls
Bare
Awakening the Trinity

The Eyes That Swallowed the Midday Sun

The Eyes That Swallowed the Midday Sun

C.L. Brown

Shadow Leaf

Published in the United States of America.

ISBN: 978-1-7350311-0-1

Thanksgiving

My feet sometimes stray, but my heart remains true to the path. The obstacles often feel overwhelming, but I am grateful for the wisdom and the strength harvested in the fight to overcome them.

I breathe, and I know you, Spirit. I shake the labored hand of the elderly and glare into the untainted eyes of the newly born, and you are wonderfully present.

I listen as the Nightingale serenades the stay of night, and you adorn my soul in immeasurable peace. My tears convey the secrets of the broken soul, because my heart carries the scars of love. Yet, I give thanks, for no man has ever known the freedom of light until he's felt the unrelenting grasp of darkness.

I am, eternally, grateful.

To My Children

I, once, saw the sun rise to dance with the moon. The sky was never, again, the same.

To my divine lights, Luna Marverly and Sunday Sky, you two are the joy of my whole life.

Luna, my moon, in case you ever wondered, your mother chose your name. She's always had this thing for the moon, she said. Said it soothes her. What a fitting name it is for you. When she asked me if we could name you Luna, I paused, and I too thought of the moon. The answer was easy. You have brought so much light into our lives. Your person is so very amazing. Your laughter is a sip of water in God's hands, and my soul thirsts so much for it.

One of my favorite things, in this world, is to watch you smile. It is just the most delightful thing to see. Whenever you smile, I smile. Though, sometimes, I hold it so deeply inside it forgets to surface on my face. Maybe it's a self-preservation thing.

My darling, I have seen your heart, and it knows the openness of your sleeve. This is how you chose to wear it. So, wear it with grace, but always be mindful to protect it. Be mindful who you allow it to shelter.

Sunday, my rising sun. I recall as a child; it was as though Sunday was the day that the other days chose to rest. It was the day families sat together around music and food as the scent of Jamaican dishes perfused the air around us. Its peacefulness hardly knew an equal. It's tranquil nature unforgettable. Until this very day, I still often look up at the sky on Sundays, and for a moment, at the very least, all my worries seem to dissipate into it. My love, you are a place I sit, in my leisure, with our Creator, and for this, I named you Sunday Sky.

You see, depending on where you are in this world, Sunday is either the seventh day of the week or the first day of the week. It is the point of infinity where the start of the circle meets its end. My darling, be infinite peace, firstly to yourself then to those that your path will lead you by.

The day will come when you'll need a place to release your worries too. When that day comes, know that you can always rest them next to mine in Sunday's sky.

My loves, if a day should ever come when my voice is a familiar, but a distant memory, know that you are pure and perfect light. Know that love isn't something you endeavor to find, because there is no time nor space nor distance between you and love. You are love, and love is you.

Know that there are things in this world that will try to convince you otherwise. When that time comes, I pray that my voice will be your reason, as your voices have been mine.

Be love to one another.
Be light to one another.
Be truth to one another.
Be sisters to one another.

Never allow a misunderstanding to displace the love between you. Argue if you must. Shout if you must. Fight if you must. But permit nothing under the sun to displace the love that exists between you.

Hug each other, purposefully.
Kiss each other, purposefully.
Speak to each other, purposefully.
And never allow the words, "I love you" to become unfamiliar with your lips.

Listen, always, to your inner self, for it is in your inner self that you will find the place your God truly dwells. Never be afraid of being your sole company. Spend time with yourselves, individually. Get to know yourselves so well that no one, at any time, will ever be able to tell you who you aren't. If you find yourselves miners of truth, know that the deeper within yourself that you find yourself the more the treasure you will uncover.

Time is a present. In time, you it will open, and you will see why it is I am so very much in love with you both.

Our God and Creator bless the entire journey that lies ahead of you both. As your father, I bless the entire journey that lies ahead of you both.

I love and adore you both, forever.

For Earl & Hyacinth Brown.

Because the fruit is never greater than the tree that nourished it.

Contents

"tell me something pretty."

something pretty?

"yes, something pretty."

Prelude

It is said, when the nightingale is seeking his love, he will sing deep into the night. Be there moon's light, be there pitch-blackness, be there rain, be there bone-chilling cold, he will sing deep into the night. You might ask, how does one know when this nightingale has found his love? Well, it is quite simple. For you see, when the nightingale has finally found his love, the nightingale ceases to serenade the darkness.

Rhapsodies of the Dawn

Interlude 1

"there's our server."
"what's his name again?"
marlon.
"that's not his name!"
i bet you a kiss.
if his name is marlon, you owe me a kiss.
"you would love that wouldn't you?"
"ok! it's a bet!"
hey, marlon!
may i have the check, please?
"sure thing! i'll be right back."

The Rising of Autumn's Sun

A mist of years has since descended
over that morning.
A gem buried miles deep in a herd of days
I seldom journey back through.

It bears a gift.
A light nearing the end of life
still piercing through the thick of things
I deemed unfit for the journey.

But I can feel it drawing me;
this wonderful sense of familiarity
lying at the dawn of a flawlessly imperfect memory.

I arrive at the precise moment the rising sun
breaks the brink of her eyes
—those oceans of liquid-hazel expanding
beyond my astonishment—

She greets me, smile first.
Then a pleasant "good morning" flees the confines
of lips that appropriates my breathing
without a measure of effort.

I take a moment to reacquaint myself.
To bask in the dawn of the most darling
of encounters.

Assuming my position as a student of her skin,
I break allegiance with my attention,
for I am enraptured by the way the rising sun
unveils the intricacies of her complexion.
You see, this woman is a balanced blend
of divinity and heritage bearing the likeness
of crude earth;
darkly rich and fertile enough that these barren
lips should conceive an adept poet.

Undoubtedly, she bears the sweetest concoction
of melanin God ever had anything to do with.

She's complementing a loosely fitted dress
that sweeps the ground with each step
as her feet proceed to bless the earth.

You would think the wind is my accomplice
the way it compels that hibiscus garden
of a garment to wrap itself around that gorgeously
petite frame of ambrosial seduction.

Her voice is the serenade of undefiled passion
reclaiming my attention.
You should hear the way it sweeps
so gracefully over me,
subduing the conversations of young lovers,
and the silence of older settlements.

Each word that she speaks sort of drifts
above the clamor of silverware and breakfast dishes,
and I am here, levitating in the ether of everything
that escapes her lips.

My heart pulsates nervous euphoria.
An unfamiliar rhythm.
I can feel it yielding to the sorcery of the grand
piano perched just inside the second story window.

Imagine, if you will, an amalgam of artful tones
harmonizing in the backdrop of your snared
attention while a spell of infallible eyes
search through the pile of things your confidence
failed to hide.

It is the sort of thing the soul cannot
come down from in the sort of morning
that gives rise to wonderful poems.

But where was I?
O yes, the air is a suave Autumn chill
suffused with the scent of aromatic desire.
The sky is unblemished blue,
and hanging on to a residue of the complete moon.
The youthful sea keeps coming and going,
busily reclaiming possessions forsaken
by higher tides.
And love, well, she's the butterfly's inaugural flight
from the cocoon of fear.

You see, I can feel her there,
in my gut,
unsettling muted emotions,
moving my very existence as my stomach flutters
at the effect of her wings.

We spend the entire morning exploring each other;

holding parts of the conversation hostage to the
silence, but our eyes refuse to stay quiet.

So, we sit closely, staring at one another,
selfishly leaving no vacancy for false pretense.

And after intimately holding hands,
we gifted the leftovers of our attention
to a candle that stood dancing in defiance
of intruding winds.

I suppose this is our way
of letting go of everything
that contests our consuming each other.

My lips keep breaking fast, partaking of hers.
And holding her strange body
in a familiar embrace,
I bless her brow with kisses that are feather-light,
and divinely textured.

It would be quite remiss of me not to mention
this tangible sense of apprehension
trying to see its way into our conversation,
but I simply cannot understand,
because nothing about this encounter feels wrong.

Quite the contrary, this is the very first morning
I've ever seen anything resembling forever
in the eyes of a woman.

And what a beautiful complement she is
to the rising of Autumn's sun.

Interlude 2

maybe we're merely embers, darling.
burning.
defying the dark.
drifting.
maybe this is us trying to find our way back
to a place we never left.

Addle the Soul

Don't you breathe, my love.
Don't you venture within.
Simply, be in the still.
Listen.

Don't you think, my love.
Don't you prostitute your thoughts
—abuse your emotions.
Don't you make any attempts to prolong the end
we've been written.

Don't you write, my love.
Don't you bastardize your heart—grieve your pen.
Don't you make any attempts to manipulate time
thinking you can squeeze one more syllable
into this line.

Don't you feel, my love.
For feelings lead to addictions,
and addictions are known to addle the soul.
Don't you make me your addiction.
Lest I become the affliction you find it impossible
to walk away from.

Don't you cry, my love.
Don't you permit a tear to erode the laughter
that we've shared together.
For I am your forever.
I am yours, forever.
So, don't you weep, my love.

Interlude 3

"i want to read your unedited poems."
why?
"because i want to see what you think of me
before you give me to the world."

Deep of Her Soul

I should tell you what I feel
when her skin ignites my erection.

I should tell you that words
and thoughts
and moderations
and restrictions
have no part of me.

I should tell you that my walls fall
each time she touches me;
each place she kisses me.

I should tell you that she is like a sun;
risen,
and perfect,
and divine.

I should tell you that serenity is a place
shrouded in the notes that she sings of me.

I should tell you that she is healing
for I have laid my ailing soul
in her tender approach to life.

I should tell you that hers is a simple touch;
the voodoo with which her flesh
summons my flesh;
filling my sleepless mind with overwhelming
emptiness.

And I should know this,
for I have lived her at night,
when beneath her wordless commands
my conquered body lied.

You see, I know her sacred place.
She's cleansed me there.
Cleansed me of old hurts
and nascent uncertainties.

Now, I see my future self
in both the shallow and the deeper end
of her now.

(Yo vivo y yo respiro en lo profundo de su alma.)
I live and I breathe in the deep of her soul.

Interlude 4

"remember the first time you kissed me
between my eyes?"
yes, i remember.
you found out you'd failed your final exam.
i could see that a good crying was beginning
to settle in your eyes,
and i wanted to get to you
before it did.
"i'd never been kissed like that before."
"no man's ever kissed me between my eyes."
"it felt strange."
"like you were herding my fears."
"i tried to resist, but i could feel my resistance
dissipating against your lips."
"all my strength left."
"my soul felt really light."
"in my mind, i whispered to death
in that moment."
what did you say to him?
"that if he'd come for me that night
he'd have gotten no fight."
well, i'm glad that he didn't come.
"me too."

Poetry in a Song's Cadence

I opine the sun merely rises to fall, again, for you.
Because had I been a sun,
that's the very thing that I would do.

I have seen the way you furnish yourself
with freedom;
habitually standing in that window each morning,
your mind naked of the day's troubles,
and your heart submissive enough
that the dawn should rest healing lips
against your consternation.

Don't you see it, darling?
I am night, and you are perfect light.
And so, on occasion, I find my person
in your arms' willingness to save discarded things.
And it feels like a conjugal dance between life
and death because we procreate a love
that is foreign to his world.

I happen to think you to be divine constellations
and cosmic disturbances,
and so, my attention has never been spent
a day away from you.

Darling, I lie with the melody that is your voice
and know the serenade of midnight storms
atop zinc-roofed shelters.

I immerse myself in the ocean of empathy
that you be, and know the depths to which
love leads the willing heart.

My wayfaring dreams all seem to coalesce perfectly
within your every waking moment.
Because, sweetheart,
you are my every waking moment.

I was asked once, "describe, for me, this woman."
From a heart engulfed in modest exuberance,
I said, she is the confluence of falling leaves,
unshackled breeze,
and purposeful gravity,
and so here I am, the one falling hopelessly.

See darling, to me, you are the poetry
hiding in a song's cadence,
and you wonder why I possess this predilection
for dancing with you.

Don't you see,
of all the homes this world has furnished me,
I chose you.
To beautify you.
To reside in you.
To erect the ruins of my world
within the conservation of your love.

So, I opine the sun merely rises to fall, again,
for you.
For had I been a sun,
that's the only thing that I would ever do.

The Birth of Autumn

I saw the birth of Autumn.
She was wearing a rising sun
and wading through a dream
painted turquoise blue.

I saw the birth of Autumn.
More peaceful than the whispers
of flirtatious willows and jovial winds,
She was a medley of festive songs
garnishing the few mundane thoughts
I keep of you.

I saw the birth of Autumn.
She was Fall's wind eroding Summer's skin.
Both beautiful and wonderful in a solitary
moment.

I saw the birth of Autumn.
She was a Nightingale's refrain
adorned in the skipping of dried leaves
over cobbled pathways;
some of the sweetest nothings ever whispered
to my transient existence.

I saw the birth of Autumn.
She was finite expressions
of boundless endearment;
a slight touch just deep enough
to compel the closing of one's eyes.

So, I closed my eyes.
And that is how I kept her inside.

So, you see, contrary to your suspicions,
I am no stranger to your petitions.
I know you adore the simplest of things;
always wanting me to tell you the prettiest things.
It was for this reason that I wrote this poem.

I wanted you to know that I have seen
the birth of Autumn,
and you,
my darling,
are something like the birth of Autumn.

Interlude 5

i keep you in a few unfinished poems.
rough drafts of sweet lies that ain't worth telling.
unpunctuated emotions.
flagrant misspellings.
surface expressions that ask nothing
of one's attention,
and yet...
yet, darling,
you are deep enough to snatch away
the breath of the curious.

i keep you in a few unfinished poems,
but there are no happy endings
to be found in them.
for you see, my darling,
the love that i carry you in it has no end,
and try as i will,
i can't think of a way to write one.

Translucent Curtains

It is my proclivity to touch her verbally.
The way I place careful words
against her fractured heart,
I hold her outside of time;
gently massaging meaningful intangibilities
into surfaced apprehensions.

I esteem her quite highly,
and so, like monuments,
and in the knowledge of her coming,
I erect metaphors completely naked
of the time we were allotted.

Applying similes like essential oils
of a sensual nature,
I baptize my tongue in her ocean
of liquid-brown melanin
while praises purposed for divine things
flee the confines of her mouth.

But she has this tendency to silence me.
The way her eyes canvas my insecurities
as she pulls me from the confinement of myself,
I know her in the seclusion of worlds
outside the infringement of material containment.

And wherever I touch her immaterial self,
she moves like a stream of water
having no knowledge of a linear path.

And it is our custom,
baring ourselves before the translucence
of curtains that are incapable of keeping secrets.

And we do this most often at night,
her vulnerabilities wedged somewhere
between an off-white wall
and frustrations I'd been dying to release.

I've told you.
I am no stranger to her sacred place.
In fact, we lie often together,
partaking of each other beneath a meddlesome
moon's sitting low in the pitch-black sky.

And that is why I adore the immersion of my fears
in her lips whispering of inaudible affirmations;
often times, in the presence of translucent
curtains.

Interlude 6

you are a setting sun's
kissing the silhouetted peeks
of distant mountains,
stargazers dressed in late summer's blossoms,
and careless sunday morning winds
grazing upon my generous skin.

don't you see, my darling,
each time that you come,
you leave me in the same
astoundingly amorous place.

Some Familiar Place I Haven't Been

When the evening found us,
we were sitting before each other,
exploring each other like tribesmen
before sacred fire.
A resident reticence in her eyes repelling the noise,
I was with a company of questions
that never left her lips,
and came to know the man that I knew
before the lies came.

We were clothed in revealing emotions;
carefully recounting the unsung stories
of our former selves.

Touching each other...
Unfolding each other like sacred poems
written on crumpled paper,
we recited one another through
unsullied intentions
and found ourselves a place
beyond temporal existence.

I remember this eager sensation
possessing me like unsheltered demons.
But being the gentleman that I am,
I spoke softly,
petitioning what remained of her fractured heart.

Her consent was the look of ambivalence
disrupting the stillness in her eyes.

Realizing, she closed them,
and so, I moved through her
like some familiar place I haven't been.

The old house was settling itself around us,
popping and squeaking like embers
of burning oak.

The room was quiet 'cept for the wooden clock
that sat ticking through time though her hands
stood frozen in it.

A mild wind had snuck through
a crack in the window
disturbing the slumber of curtains
that stood like watchmen.

And she,
my wordless poem,
was something of a divine scripture
written in the silence that occupied my mouth.

And so, in a moment stolen from the time
God has yet conceived,
I felt my tongue taming the apprehensive nature
of new beginnings.

You see, she was the charming modesty
of simple words and I the poet striving
to free the things the silence sentenced
to her spirit.

But before I knew it,

her lips began to descend upon my lips,
and my lungs began to surrender beneath
the gravity of her dominion.

She was a timely displacement of the darkness.
A much-needed vacancy.
Therapy.

And so, we conversed well into the night;
hushed mouths and jubilant eyes laughing
between the moments we cried.

You see, I have been the understudy of solitude.
A well-intended recipient of what she's taught me
—lessons on the nature of what it means
to be free—
but that night taught me there is much liberty
in the company of confessing hearts
and unshackled minds.

And so it was, we were sitting before each other,
reciting each other through meaningful sentiments.
Baptized in the resident reticence,
wisdom and compassion was our repast that night.

Interlude 7

i adore the way white sheets contrast
your darkest secrets.
the way rainy mornings find us at the end
of moonlit nights.
your lips.
your eyes.
the way i surrender my strength
between your thighs.
darling, i adore the way white sheets contrast
your darkest secrets.

Wasteland

Won't you let me be your wasteland?
The place you cast away days
you'd rather nights
not remember.

Won't you let me be the solitude
that finds you in crowded rooms?
The place your thoughts will run to
when you'd rather be away.

Won't you let me be the silence
that takes your voice away?
The place that always listens
to the things you'd rather not say.

Won't you, darling?
Won't you let me be your wasteland?

Interlude 8

i woke up this morning,
and before the world occupied
a morsel of my mind,
i indulged a wonderful thought of you.
my love, how are you?
"hmmm ... a bit up and down."
you know, ups and downs are clear signs
of a healthy life cycle.
suns rise and they fall.
so do moons.
and you carry the essence
of the heavens within you,
so, you will too.
"well, that's just the most beautiful
tuesday morning poem i've ever heard."
almost as beautiful
as your tuesday morning voice,
i suppose.
(smiles)
"i like that."

Gift of Night

While the moon kept watch of the sun,
I rose from a dream and found my being
lying between a rainstorm
and a pleasing memory of you.

It was 3 a.m. again.
A gift.
Not one I deserved,
but God's goodness is God's goodness,
and I am no one to contend.

So, I smiled a soft rapturous glow.
I held it with my heart though the darkness
protested into the night.

You then dipped your presence
into my drowsy musings, commencing
a rippling of—otherwise—dormant desire.
So, I gave my attention to the intonations
of your voice, then melted into the sheets,
a lasting residue of you.

A few thoughts staggered haphazardly
into my honesty.
A song by any other name.
But you lulled my turbulent mind
with hushed lips and wordy eyes;
a quiet surrender.
A habitation that implored my soul to bare itself.
And it bared itself.

Interlude 9

"do you love me?"
i do.
"unconditionally?"
no, imperfectly.
"what does that even mean?"
there is no such thing as unconditional love,
my love.
if love can be unconditional then naturally
it can also be conditional.
but love cannot be conditional.

so, there is just love,
and all expressions of it are flawed
in one way or the other.
so, yes, imperfectly,
i love you with every single breath
that i take or don't take.
"where did you come from?"
i am here, and i am yours.
what else matters?

Interlude 10

out there,
in the world,
you were merely a storm.
careless,
misunderstood,
wild.
but in here,
in the enclosure of these poems,
you are the serenade of thunder,
of lightning,
and the soft humming of late-night raindrops
on the other side of my window.

Breathe You In

Have you ever noticed how the prying moon
looks down on you?
How she disrobes herself against your skin
each time the darkness takes all but your voice
away from me?

Heaven is your lip's revelation of your smile
whenever your confidence tries to excuse itself.

O, woman, I have seen dimensions of you
wherein words have no gravity.
Perspectives that make it impossible to address
a future that is naked of you.

But you hide behind those eyes
as though there is a world outside
waiting to get you.

But no, my love.
There is no world out there.
It is only I, right here.
Right here waiting for you
to reveal what lies beyond that gorgeous skin
that I may show you the very reason
I am still here,
still waiting,
still longing,
still dying,
to breathe you in.

Interlude 11

while she spoke of childhood dreams,
the mid-morning's breeze took pieces
of the emptying of her soul out to sea,
and i sat there basking in my glee
wandering in the deep
of intermittent silence.

Moon Lights My Sky

I have seen the way the morning
dawns in your eyes,
but touching you in the night's reluctance
to hold the moon,
now there's a reason to cease one's breathing.

I have seen weeping clouds come together
like broken loved ones do.
How they fall as they sing
in the background of my loving you.

It is hell being confined to your absence,
but I make something good of the few memories
you left while hand-crafted instruments
set the tone and the texture of my rapture.

Darling, it was always an out-of-body experience
witnessing your touch confiscating my breath.

But there are no hands left to touch me now.
No lips left to heal me now.
No love left to free me now.

So, I search no more.
Not for answers.
Not for questions.
Not for reasons.
I search no more.

Interlude 12

i don't know a place on your skin
that the sun hasn't been.
i envy that.

Last Days in Havana

I am here.
I am sitting in the shadow of your calm.
Only the bare necessities.

Your wild eyes under the spell of the falling sun.
My captive eyes under the spell of you.

Celia Cruz is lamenting loveless illusions
while Cuban fishermen tackle a restless sea
under the spell of Caribbean winds.

The evening is approaching so delicately,
and there is a beauty on this balcony
that only muses and poets can embody.

The silhouette of your partially veiled body
transcribing the most beautiful poetry.

And these...
These are the last days in Havana.

Interlude 13

i had kissed you a thousand times,
and yet your mouth knew not the taste of truth.
you deserved that.
you deserved it,
and that is why my last kiss was in the company
by a conspicuous goodbye.
i knew it wasn't what you wanted to feel,
but it was honest.
it was honest,
and you deserved that.

The Eyes That Swallowed the Midday Sun

When I bared myself to God,
she was midnight black
and with eyes that swallowed
the midday sun.

Arrayed in both my past and my present,
she was a beauty as pure as the darkness
that hasn't known light,
and yet, she was the dawning of light.

Her voice was home,
and music,
and crackling wood in fireplaces,
strings and acoustic melodies,
winds and chimes conversing,
quietude and the dispelling of useless thought.

Memories I had not lived she drew from me
the way water summons life from the dying seed.

When she gave me permission,
I entered her person.
When I left, I was in need of nothing.

She ushered me into her morning
and caused the wind to perfume of lavender
and freshly cut jasmine.

I closed my eyes then breathed her in.
Salvation.

She slipped her tongue between my lips
divulging parabolic secrets.
Elevation.

She was an ocean of tears and I, an emptied soul.
And so, she cried.
And so, I sipped.
Redemption.

When I bared myself to God,
she was midnight black
and with eyes that swallowed
the midday sun.

Interlude 14

you are the fire that sits
upon my candle's wick.
both the light
and the life of my soul
in the very same instance.

Not in Vain

It is the most delicate thing I've come to know,
the nature of a flower.
The first time I saw her,
she was in a safe space,
someplace between a mild wind
and my untarnished devotion.
Unwittingly flirting with my attention,
she bared herself for love
and not in vain.

She was adorned in colors
my eyes have not seen in one place.

A gift of earth.
A darling in the company of imperfections,
she was torn petals and premature blossoms
embellishing the ground that consoled my feet.

She was evidence of the abuse time
and circumstance often leave behind,
but the poetry in my eyes when I saw her
was the courtship of souls naked of agendas.

She was a generosity that's never been reciprocated.
A pure lesson in love and its essence
of unblemished sacrifice.

Yes, she was broken,
in fact, a few petals missing,
but she held my attention
as though it was priceless.

And as I stood there in the charming stillness,
yielding my will in an ocean of gratitude,
she danced gracefully with the wind,
not even a single word spoken.

She was swaying somewhere between my soul
and my skin as though I were the faultless rays
of a rising sun.

That was her way of emptying herself,
and I was no fool.
So, I took her in slowly and carefully
as not to violate her acceptance
of my presence.

And bathing in the spillage of her silence,
I bared myself to love
and not in vain.

Interlude 15

"what is it that you want from me?"
your first good mornings
and your last good nights,
for the rest of my life.

Beautiful, You Always Are

Beautiful you are.
Light.
A gentle wind always in my company.
A teacher, compassionately.
A lover defying the erosive nature of time.

Time, I deny this at your fingers' tips.
Smiling at the words your eyes siphon
from your soul.
Acquiescing to the besieging of your arms
about my apprehension.
You subdue me, darling,
and yet, there is no fight
in the nature of your touch.

Love, you see, isn't something that you do well.
Love, my darling, is the very essence
of a moment spent lingering in the air
of your existence.

You are light, my love.
You are light.
And beautiful, you always are.

Shelter

I keep a place between my lips
for your tongue to be.
I see the weight of your secrets
each time you open your eyes to me.

I see how well you carry them.
How you hold them like precious children.
But I promise you, they are safe inside me, too.

So, allow yourself the freedom.
This fall into my possession.
Such a simple act of submission,
but its parallel lies only in the heart
that I use to carry you.

Come, let me show you the place
I grew to love you.
Let me show you,
though I've kept it vacant,
it has no room to hurt you.

The sun rises here,
but it does not displace the darkness.
For what are we but perennial darkness
arrayed in ephemeral light.

You are and have always been my light.
So, what have I if you can't reveal it?
And what am I if you can't declare it?

You have made of secrets your blanket,
but I am here to cover you now.
You have made of solitude your prison,
but I am here to free you now.

So, let us not make light of this poem,
and it will be a fixture in the night
that we stripped love bare and knew her intimately.

And let us not make waste of this bed,
and it will be a place your secrets are shed
that I may see you, finally.

So, promise me you won't hold your screams,
for me.
And promise me you won't close your legs, to me.

Promise you won't imprison the tears
that came to set you free.
And promise you won't let this night find you
come morning, without me.

Interlude 16

i'm lying here watching time
pile on top of me,
and it makes me realize
that whatever it is i was to you
has long ago been buried.
but even so,
tonight, you are somewhere
beneath the same sky as i am.
maybe you're close by.
maybe you're far away.
but wherever you are,
i know you're somewhere
beneath the same sky as i am,
and baby, well, that's close enough for me.

To Whom Much Is Given

A tiny bird sang for me this morning.
So many beautiful places in this world.
So many beautiful faces,
but she sat where my heart
and my eyes were vacant,
and she sang, just for me.

When it was over,
the gray sky weeping for the absent sun,
behind her.
"How may I repay you?" I whispered.
But she would answer in silence
gazing my direction.

She sat until I'd emptied my heart
of fruitless questions.
Then I too sat in flawless silence.

But time would be generous
and she would give her wings to the waiting wind.
Then the waiting wind would give itself
to my skin.
Then I would be compelled to release
all that I had taken in.
Because you would be here this day inhaling this
poem.

Interlude 17

when you found me,
i was rooted in self-serving agendas
and bearing fruit that you could not digest,
but i watched you eroding a bit more
of my ego each time your eyes wandered
unabashedly around my face.
now i can't think anything of myself
without thinking everything of you.

The Way You See the Sea

You say my attention seems divided.
That I am always coming and going
as though my loyalty knows two masters.

But what you don't seem to know
is that I've seen the way
the sea takes hold of you.

How you lose your way in her chaos
to find your calm.
How she drowns your fears
and leaves you with a peace
that makes death of no consequence.

How she comes to you.
How she washes your feet as if to undo
the mess you've been through.

How before long she pulls away from you
only to come again when she sees fit.
But you sit.
You wait.
And while you wait, you exude a patience
I can only transcribe as divine.

So, you see,
all this time,
I have only wanted you
to lose yourself to me
the way you lose yourself to the sea.

I have only wanted to hold you;
to kiss the bruises on your feet as if to undo
the hardships you've been through.

I have only wanted
that when I go away
you would wait for me
the way you wait for the sea.

So, you see, I have been your sea.
Chaotic and free.
Consoling though inconsistent.
Adoring though sometimes overbearing.

But it doesn't matter what I have been.
It doesn't matter, darling.
Because you will never see me.
Not the way you see the sea.

Interlude 18

"do you think you'll love me forever?"
well, love has no life for death to take from it.
'course, i could always choose to bury it,
but wouldn't that be a crime.

The Place You Shall Not Fall From

That fear desires freedom,
and I am your wings.

Campfires burn brighter
in sheets of midnight's blackness.

I see you suspended in impenetrable darkness.
But, my darling,
I am the place you shall not fall from.

I saw your wind-swept embers
being raptured against my night's sky.

And your light rose over my day come morning.

You always knew how to keep the cold
from my naked skin.
And so darling,
I am the place you shall not fall from.

Interlude 19

by the way,
the look in your eyes,
how they unfold your soul
each time our lips touch each other,
its parallel still hasn't found a place
in this world.

Falling Stars and Rising Moons

Some hearts are seduced by falling stars
and rising moons.
But the thing that makes me weak
is my arms around the things
you never share with this world.

I remember that evening.
Your past was your prison,
but the present sky,
that masterpiece of Time,
it was your reflection.
I saw you then when the ocean's wind
eroded your apprehensions.
You were the scent of incipient love
and the answer to everything I did not deserve.

But you trusted me.
You trusted me as though I hadn't broken
a few precious things in my time.
The ocean was kind.
She kept consoling us every few seconds.
Each time the deep taking more of us
through the very same window.

You were the essence of surrendered inhibitions,
and sweetly so.
I was the pulse of your life.
I felt you inside.
Your soul was in the audience of mine,
and my attention was center stage.

We were drifting in the sound of seabirds
serenading the orange twilight;
a faint but delightful addition to the whispers
of breaking waves.

Your breathing was paced.
Your body molded into submission.
The ocean kept coming and going,
saturating the secrets my lips
were burying between your thighs.
And time was only innocently by standing,
but o how we abused her.

I remember how you navigated my silence
like a poet's tongue in a sea of words;
how you appropriated my strength
as though I wasn't already yours.

We were expressions of honesty written
on sheets of muted sand.
Me reading the questions residing on your lips.
You kissing the answers fleeing from mine.

You have since been the gift of time,
a native of my soul,
and I will never gift you to another.
I know I sold you many lies since that evening,
but you should know it was the time of my life
watching from your delicate eyes,
the moon rising in a company of falling stars.

Interlude 20

some days the breeze hits you
with the remains of a past life.
today it was pieces of your smile
scattered among promises i broke.
it was lies i spoke to waste more of your time.
it was shame.
it was regret.
it was tear tracks that led me back
to the place i left you.

Always Been With You

I watch the skies turn at night.
Because its lights know the kindness of your eyes.

My heart knows the depths of the heavens.
And it has always been with you.

Her touch was everything.
But my thirst found death upon your lips.

My heart knows the depths of the heavens.
And it has always been with you.

Your arms welcomed me like open meadows.
And my fears became cocoons I flew from.

My heart knows the depths of the heavens.
And it has always been with you.

My intentions took refuge in the silence.
But we moved in the prayers of midnight violins.

My heart knows the depths of the heavens.
And it has always been with you.

Interlude 21

it's raining today.
and your essence lingers.
there is some consolation in knowing
i'm not alone to weather this grief.
you see, the sky, too, misses you.

The Sun Didn't Come With the Evening

The sun didn't come with the evening.
But I hold you so close.

The blackbirds mock me in the distance.
But the nightingales won't have the darkness
to swallow me whole.

The blooming flowers wilt as I read this poem.
But they dance in the wind as though death
is some ways out.

My mind is nowhere close to me.
Buy my heart flirts with the nearness of you.

So, darling, don't you see?
The sun didn't come with the evening.
But the evening surely did come
with the presence of you.

Songbirds and Midday Rains

Interlude 22

you can be so cold.
quiet.
but you carry a fireplace for a soul,
and that...
that is what makes you home.

Sin Distraction

You wonder about the places I spend my attention,
but it has always lied with you,
my beautiful addiction.
Why else do you suppose I've numbered the lines
that form in the corners of your eyes
each time that you smile?
Why do you suppose I can detect the inflections
in your voice right before a lie escapes your lips?

I have seen the way passing moons reflect
off that glorious melanin while you lied freely
in my possession.
Vulnerable positions.
Heaven.

You displace my darkness, so well.
Your nakedness at my fingers' tips.
Your emancipation's proclamation
at the tip of my oscillating tongue.
The encapsulation of unborn time in your eyes
and the way they search the void I call my soul.
Divination.

But tonight, your body's a complete distraction.
Now, don't misunderstand.
For the way you carry yourself in that skin,
my mind,
my heart,
they stand entirely nude.

Darling, I have been your willing captive
since that first night I witnessed a new moon's rise
in those mud-brown eyes.

You gave me permission then to enter in;
to find your soul in the mess life's made of it.
Well, I did, and I haven't left.

So, tonight, won't you undress yourself?
Won't you allow our conversation to birth
conversations until we both come out from hiding?

Tonight, won't you let time petition
for our attention as we become the subjects
of each other's meditation?
Darling, tonight, won't you let me, have you?
Won't you let me have all of you,
sin distraction?

Interlude 23

today is the darkest day i've known.
the sky is weeping too.
i have words needing speaking.
they need healing too.

Owes Nothing to Time

The morning I fell for you lives in a memory
that owes nothing to time.
The sky was perfect if you can believe anything
could ever be.

A generous breeze had come along bringing with it
the first breath of Autumn.
Fall's leaves were shedding Summer's skin.
The clouds had excused themselves leaving
no obstruction in the path of the rising sun.

I remember the charm of wind-swept palms
and an impassioned bluebird casting spells
just beyond my window.

Your lips and your fingers were stirring questions
while a swarm of goose pimples narrated
the texture of your touch.

You were blank pages,
and I was an eagerness waiting to scribble
heartfelt prose and breathtaking poems
all over them.

It was the type of morning nights often dream of.
Powerless eyes disrobed of shame
and provocative thoughts discarding silence.

Old sheets were stained with contemporary love
and wrinkled in all the places we depleted
one another.

I remember collecting my words
like the shattered pieces of a prayer
that refused to ascend.

That morning, I laid out my heart
—a rug stained crimson pain—
before feet that weren't worthy to walk over me.

I never imagined the night would come
when you would walk over me.
But still, I carry that morning in a memory
that owes nothing to time.

Interlude 24

"what will tomorrow say about us?"
it will be jealous.
"jealous of what?"
jealous of today.
"why is that?"
because what we're sharing with today
won't make it through the night.

Entirely Still

Often, when both the sun and his moon
go off into hiding,
when the naked sky resembles the ebony G-string
my lips removed from your cocoa skin,
I think of that Nightingale's serenade.
How gorgeously he sang while rainclouds
set the tone for love's making.

I think of your pieces,
and I think of my pieces;
how beautifully they coalesced into
the broken mess that gave us purpose.

I think of the divine interludes
of profane expletives that rolled off your tongue
while mine rendered you strengthless.

Since you left,
I often correspond with the pain,
but she never answers.
So, the letters pile up like dead bodies
in mass graves.
Guess, I truly stink at this.

But I pray someday I will inhale, again,
the excesses of life escaping your abundance.

That I'll see the way darkness touches
your melanated skin after the partial moon
had risen.

That I'll lie naked with your sheltered heart,
while submitting to the jurisdiction
of your faultless eyes.

And if that day should come,
I will offer to God what I kept from you.
An honest word.
Then I will lie down with time
the way I will lie down with you.

Completely freed of the lies.
And entirely, still.

Interlude 25

i'm sorry that i can't seem to do right by you.
i try to keep my heart in a good place,
at least the parts i keep you in.
but no matter how far away you run,
it always leads me back to hurting you.
"it's ok."
"the poet is sacred ground,
but oftentimes a haunted place."
so, then are you not afraid?
"darling, fear is a stimulus only for those
who haven't slept with the darkness."

No Room for You

There is forgiveness in your eyes.
So, I have no business inside of them.

They have a tendency to shed tears
that I am unworthy of.
Often bloodshot and saturated with a measure
of pain no single person should ever have
to burden.

When we kissed with the last dishonest goodbye
that sat between my lips,
you asked me why.

Why it was I chose to hurt the heart
that only wanted to heal.
Why it was you were looking into my eyes,
but could no longer find your place inside of them.
Why it was you no longer existed
at the tip of my pen.

I felt the weight of those words
though I couldn't help you to carry them.
And I broke for you as if you had the room
to break anymore.

Then I began searching myself.
I was searching the flagrant lies that had
your stomach teaming with butterflies.
I was searching my own eyes and learned that truth
has no such companion.

I was searching the pieces of the promises
I had deliberately broken.

I was even imagining my lips between your thighs,
your moistened skin caressing the tip of my chin,
your flow and your flower's glow as you blossomed
at the tip of my tongue,
but I felt nothing.

All that searching and the only thing I found
was that my heart was vacant where you were
concerned.

I knew your sole ambition was to meet me
where you were standing,
and so, you waited,
and you waited,
but the truth is,
darling,
I was always running.

Interlude 26

the most liberating thing i've ever done
was erasing your name,
the hundred or so times that i wrote it.

I Break

I break.
Like a piece of priceless porcelain
falling from fallible hands,
I break.

I fall to the ground.
But I make no sound.
You aren't much around
to absorb my pain anyway.

I break.
Like a fragile heart caught in lustful complications.
My pieces lie at your feet,
and you've never been the kind
to regard the things you place beneath them.

But don't you worry, darling.
This day will be swept up in your wind
of indifference much like my pieces will.

Then someday,
someone,
somewhere,
will gather together
what you couldn't hold together.

One-by-one my pieces will find a home
in stranger hands.
See, to you, I am only glimpses and glitters
of the things you failed to be,
but they will see something worth saving
in the nothingness that you think me to be.

So, I break away from you,
though it is breaking me.

And though I look towards the uncertainty
that is tomorrow,
I am certain that you will never live to see
a today quite like me again.

Because I break, darling.
But it is in this,
my breaking,
that lies everything I'll ever need to mend.

Outcast

I held the moon,
but her scars felt unfamiliar.
I saw her aged memories,
those things she cherished most.
But me, I wasn't there.

Interlude 31

in the beginning,
we held conversations so beautiful
i thought flowers grew from them.
it was my favorite thing watching you
sauntering through pictures my words painted,
stopping at all the places
your image of me hadn't yet faded.
sometimes, through silence, i'd pour you
everything my heart kept.
sometimes, we'd meet in the quiet spaces
between the speaking,
and it reminded me death hadn't come my way yet.
but as wonderful as it has been,
i fear our end will be marred with waning faces
and the distance of voices shrouded
in unyielding contempt.
"death doesn't come for those who don't have
a life to give it, darling."
what do you mean?
"i mean, if we don't leave anything for an end,
what reason has an end to come?"
you're right.
but if it does come,
it will have to pry you from my cold stiff hands.
"i love you."
i know.

Abandoned Purpose

You are the dust housing the furnishings
of my former self.
Merely fragments of unspoken apologies,
I have become but cemented circumstances
and abandoned purpose.

I was sifting through us,
opening my fears like drawers and doors
your fingers' prints no longer smear.

I found you there.
Broken and beautiful;
face down in the fetal position,
your knees attempting to stabilize
the back-and-forth swaying of your chest
as you endeavored to collect what was left
of your fractured heart.

You were hiding behind words I spoke
that you couldn't get past.
Your freedom anchored in a shallow pool
of shattered confidence while your worth of self
drifted like the wreckage of sunken hope.

I held my hands out, but they were as empty
as the promises I filled your mind with.
I begged you to come with me
—o the selfish pleas of unmeasured desperation—
but you just sat there.
Waiting, but not waiting.

Contempt for me pouring from your eyes
as you analyzed the gravity of my resignation.

I began to retract my hands just as the swaying in
your chest began to fade.
See, I knew this was your moment
—your walking away from your monster—
and I envied you for it.
Because, unlike you,
I can't walk away from me.

With time, the tears would cease to flow,
as hope found its place on distant shores.
Your mouth would open to free some things,
but my name would not be found among them.
You would mend,
where I would break.
And purpose would become a victim
of circumstance as you gave space
to the waning silence.

Water

I have no thirst for pain today.
So, your tears do not excite me.

I feel no inclination towards empathy.
So, your need of validation will not be met.

I know you long for the mess you left.
The comfort.
Because that's home, isn't it?
But, you see, after you left
I rearranged a few things.
You did say I was too much.
So, I threw out a few things.

You were drowning, you said, and I was like water.

So, you left, and the days grew long,
and I grew confused.
But one day, in searching your absence,
the pain led me to someone else.
And this someone else, she was thirsty.
She was thirsty, and I was like water.
I was like water,
but I was everything she needed me to be.

So, I thank you.
Because, you see, you taught me a drowning man
may not care for the life-saving nature of water,
but as it turns out, the life he seeks to save
cannot live without it either.

Interlude 32

i am afraid too,
but i see something inside of you
that all of the fear in the world, combined,
could never muscle away from me.
so, if it be that life must lead you away,
then i will wade in the desolation of death.
for, surely, the darkness has something left
of the nights that we shared with it.

When No One Is Around to Listen

Self-reflection had a way of revealing his demons.
Heartfelt words.
Misunderstood expressions.
The pain seemed most articulate
when no one was around to listen.

She fell against and seeped into his soul
like rainfall on porous soil.
Then she grew from him a beautiful poem
and like flowers burgeoning from the lips
of the earth.

She made of him a slave to her freedom,
her audience in his demons,
but he refused to abort childlike intentions
because pain is the firstborn of sheltered hearts
and feral emotions.

But it was all perfect that morning.
The new sun's gentle rise in her eyes
and how pleasantly they swallowed him.
The violin serenading the ceremony of his falling.
The high hopes birthed of silly expectations.
The aroma of cheap coffee and last goodbyes
decorating the empty table where they held
similar conversations.

The day came with copious rain,
but he couldn't wash her away.

For when her brown eyes confiscated his attention,
she mowed over his emotions then proceeded
to wear him like some sort of fragrance,
priceless and foreign like the formless poem
she couldn't comprehend.

They'd seen greener pastures,
but those rains had since moved on.
All he had left were the remnants
of malnourished poems disclosing the bones
he kept hidden inside his closet.

He'd decorated his soul for her,
but all she ever did was walk leisurely over it.

Self-reflection has a way of revealing his demons.
Heartfelt words.
Misunderstood expressions.
The pain is always most articulate
when no one is around to listen.

Interlude 33

and if you ever truly loved me,
please, don't release me.
not yet.

Shadowy Figures and Fading Echoes

When the remorse finally caught up to me,
I was in a strange place being displaced
by a familiar poem.

Barely holding together my divided attention,
I was halfway down a glass of brown rum
clutched in my right hand,
flipping through naked thoughts of you,
undressing you,
while you slowly stripped me away from your time.

It is safe to say that I was intoxicated,
because I kept regurgitating this sinking feeling
of you walking away from me once again.

When I couldn't bear the thought
of another second of another day away from you,
the residue of brown rum pervading my tongue
like your brown skin used to do,
I parted ways with myself in the most selfish way.

By the time the pride caught up to me,
my hands were pleading,
screaming at your door;
my famished soul hoping and praying
that your heart was still open.

A few moments later, you opened wearing only
a see-through thong and that delicious caramel
addiction you called your skin.

For a second, I lost sight of our present situation.
Falling victim to the familiarity of my addiction,
I began to drift in the subtle illusion,
touching you like my fingers were strangers
to your skin.

And with a full-bodied moon keeping vigil,
I kissed your smile proving love is impervious
to delusions of distance and time.

But then just like that, I pulled myself back
from the edge of the moment.
My tongue saturated with intoxicated words,
I was scripting a greeting inside my head
while my hands wiped the sadness from my eyes.
See, I was desperately trying to compose myself.

"May I come in?"
A piece of my fractured heart managed to slip
past the pride revealing longings I was
—nine months—hiding,
awaiting your permission.

But you refused to let me back in.
Dangling my addiction before my eyes,
you said I'd become nothing but blurred lines
and unwelcomed visits.

I began to break the moment those lies parted
your tear-soaked lips, but that pride realized
and stood guard before my eyes.

So, I just stood there in the waning optimism
watching the anger inhabiting more room
inside of you.

We began shouting at each other
because broken hearts seldom whisper.

And I watched you watching the lies in my eyes
taking sides while pride got the very best
of me again.

It has since been three years, my darling,
and I still haven't managed to remove myself
from your door.

Sometimes, I try to visit the reasons we became us,
but there's only you and me and those distant
memories now.

And though I know the way back to you,
I also know the indecisions that I used
to forge your prison.

I know the clear signs written in confusion;
the potholes lining the roadways where teardrops
and I parted ways.

So, though I'm dying to breathe you in again,
to succumb to that addiction you call your skin,
my feet refuse to take directions from my heart
again.

But I'm still possessed by those monstrous
emotions.
The ones that kept me fettered to the illusions.
That tumultuous calm I weathered inside
your eyes.
The pretty lies.
The unbridled words my lips could no longer
reign over.

And though I still know what it feels like
to hold you, we are but shadowy figures
and fading echoes now.

For you see, there was never a place
for lucent sentiments in those black holes
you called eyes,
but still, I rose, always and only, for them;
if only to fall again for the way they snared
that transient sun.

I still remember that broken reflection
gazing back that night while I displaced
myself inside of them.
O, but it's been quite some time
since I've seen that man.

I still remember that devil inside of you, too.
The same one that occupied your duplicitous
tongue.
I remember offering my trust
and my undefiled devotion,
but as much as it burned,
my sacrifice was never pleasing.

In the end, you were left to stand on precarious
promises while I walked away the man
that kept your mind closed and your legs opened.

I left when the night grew confusing,
but never came back when daylight offered
the chance to clear things up.

So, I'm sorry, my darling.
For though I'm still possessed
by the same emotions,
those monsters that kept me fettered
to the illusions, we are but shadowy figures
and fading echoes now.

Black Sea

The black sea still calls me.
Her voice still touches me more intimately
than the impassioned wind—caresses me
more tenderly than the expanse of time
in the hands of grace.

Her present ways are displacements
of lingering solitude.
Her elderly ways, the serenade of juvenile
sentiments.

Whenever I find myself a prisoner of unsolicited
reasoning, she exfoliates my thinking like
aging skin.

She's shown me things she's never shared
with the sun.
I still carry them the way unsettled arguments
carry the stench of resentments.

I know the peace that persists in her company,
because for so many days, and in so many ways,
she's permitted me to lie freely in her stillness.

Not even God at his best has ever held me
in such stillness.

The black sea still calls me.
And she's been my counselor.
And she's been my lover.

She's been my song and its instrument.
And I've always admired the way her reticence
masticates words before she ever allowed me
to ingest even the tiniest bit of her.

And she's got this way of oscillating
between my past and my present
in such a way that reminds me,
though love feels sometimes absent,
she's never not felt familiar.

And you should see the way mid-aged moons
and sunless skies cast shadows and lights
against her.
The way my boldest endeavors and deepest fears
stumble through her darkness like novel love
in older hearts.

The black sea still calls me.
Some nights she whispers enticements
that leave my soul like clear minds
in confused conversations.
Some days her lips spill wisdom and compassion
like mountains do water at the birth of spring.

Like diluvial rainbows on the path
to divine promises,
her tranquil ways are indelible reminders
that my best days are yet ahead of me.

The black sea still calls me.
And so, I still run to her, naked,
but never ashamed.

I am never ashamed.
Because the black sea, she still loves me.

Interlude 34

"do you fear sadness?"
sadness?
i don't fear sadness at all.
not anymore.
"how come?"
i've spent too much time with him.
you spend enough time with a monster
and fear will eventually wear out its welcome.
he's not so bad once you get to know him.
besides, he listens well.
and well, sometimes you need that.
"need what?"
someone to listen.

Between the Times

The feel of you is sunlit Sunday mornings
laved in the mild rain of transitory clouds;
the sound of you the praise of evening birds;
the sight of you is the rippling of waters disclosing
the pathways of clandestine winds.

You are the comfort of home,
friendship,
and leisurely music pacifying the anxiety
that defiles the soul.

You are a nascency very well esteemed,
yet I feel there is no time that has ever found me
away from you.

I come to you always in passing,
most often while the naked sky grieves
her fallen sun.
And each morning that you see me off,
I leave behind articles of myself,
because narcissistic ways will always
lead me back to your bed.

So, don't you fret, my darling.
Don't you permit fear a night's stay in your heart,
for fear has been known to dampen the glory
of courageous things.

I know in our encounters you conceived questions
that never begot answers.
I know that you lied freely,
openly to my absence,
because hope is the sustenance of a love
that craves the arms that will hold her back.

I know that I cycle through your cycles unchanged,
yet unfamiliar.
And each time that we've made love,
you've said the light of the moon held you anew,
and yet, there are no eyes that know the sky
before she adorned it.

So, do not grieve my absence as though
my presence has a place outside of it.

Let me go, my love, for only then can that
old moon hold you like new again.

But before I go, please darling,
kiss me like your purpose.
Hold me like your reason.
For as surely as I go,
like that old moon,
and in due season,
I will come, and I will hold you anew again.

Interlude 35

sometimes, the gift of freedom
is a smudgy window in your tiny cell.
perhaps the empty meadow has something
a cage full of you never did.
hope.

i, often, run freely through unwritten reveries
still anchored to apparitions of you.

sometimes, the gift of freedom
is a smudgy window in your tiny cell.
i find my way out now and again,
but you always manage to find your way in.

Habitual Rituals

We found refuge inside a curbside coffee shop.
It was hidden on an Autumn Georgian
Sunday morning just beyond the reach
of summer's end.
Truly, it was the ideal season for love, of any kind,
to blossom.

If I should be honest, we felt amiss;
lost, in fact, but not quite wanting to be found.

So, we sat cuddled between cobwebbed corners;
holding each other beneath a couple
of dust-covered lanterns that stood waning
in the clement rise of the infant sun.

The sky outside was marble-blue and sprinkled
with a few scattered clouds.
The rain was a light veil of country-side comfort,
but the daffodils sitting on the windowsill
might had well been confined to a cell.

Nestled between a muted wall
and a tsunami of foreign conversations,
a strange woman was playing a familiar tune,
and we only strolled through composed fields
of lively bluegrass.

She was so graceful, this woman,
the way she displaced escorted solitude.

With her insistent tune was plowing through
calloused memories, I was quietly excavating
precious relics of you.

With nostalgic emotions being bared
in visibly desolate eyes,
I, so badly, wanted to be alone.
To escape habitual rituals
and brave the haunting feeling
of dying to make of you a home again.

While we sat, I went back to the night
I witnessed my eyes displacing tears
to make room for you.
The night my heart siphoned fear from my soul
so my flesh would know what it feels like
when giants fall.

But then somewhere between loving you
and being free;
between the foreign tongues and local aromas'
saturation of saddened sentiments;
between the cries of mahogany floors
and the cadence of walnut chairs
dancing over them;
between philosophized conversations
and the intermittent silence we took refuge in;
romanticizing the past in an adulterous attempt
at being intimate again with the quiet place
between your leisured breathing,
I witnessed the thunderous inception
of her quiet love.

Engrossed by the way her soft lips shaped
hard words, I was edaciously feasting
on the innocence her eyes brought to the table.

Her smile could light the entirety of any room,
but it failed to penetrate my darkness
the way your selfish frown used to do.

The body of conversations we were immersed in
—revealing places your lips had previously been—
was but the transcription of the language lucid
and native to her soul.

She made me feel so free.
Her aspirations mended my broken wings
because her present situation was ignorant
of my intentions of flying back to you.

But I know now what the infancy
of love looks like.
What it feels like.
What it sounds like.
How selfless and hopeless.
How open and innocent.
How pure and breathtakingly beautiful.

Even so, she doesn't know that I won't be around
to see us grow.
Oh no!
She doesn't know that I'll go back
to the habitual rituals of displacing tears,
because I still need to make more room for you.

Interlude 36

does the poet's heart belong to another?
is it not to be free?
i know i am only your caged bird,
and though i know not the taste of such delicacy,
i know no other pleasure
than to watch you
savoring the peace of my pain.

you revel in my elegies.
you sleep to my serenade,
and i will sing unto death
before i cause your rest to conclude.
on the rare occasion,
you'll touch me,
but merely out of possession;
not ever of desire.
so, tell me,
does the poet's heart belong to another?
is it not to be free?
why, then, won't you set me free?

To Have Me Is to Lose Me

You wish me to yourself.
How foolish the heart.
You bind me with your spell.
The monster in your circle of influence.
You feel free when you are with me because
delusions are but projections of the untethered
mind.

It breaks me to know that one day
you will release me, then you too shall break.

I allow my lips to fall on you in diverse places
because you fascinate my being with your
reception of words.

Your mouth causes my flesh to feel life.
When I kiss you, you say, "God speaks life."

You would give the world—you say—
for the fleeting feeling of my lips
against your skin again.
And so, you wish me to yourself,
though it was my freedom that permitted you
to partake of me.

So, you see, to have me is, in fact, to lose me.
Because movement is life, my dear.
Both my coming and my going are your gifts.
So, allow me to present you with my absence.
For to have me is to lose me, my dear.

Hated Most

Funny,
it was my silence you hated most,
but that is where I learned to love you,
most.

Funny,
you made words so unnecessary.
I have read your eyes countless times.
That is how I learned the texture of your story.
So, you learned to hate my silence most,
but that is where I learned to touch you,
most.

Funny,
you shed your clothes regularly,
so easily,
in front of me.

Now and again, I noticed the way you placed
your hand to my chest as though trying
to interpret the things my heart hadn't yet written.

My eyes were seldom open
whenever we allowed love the freedom
of expression.
So, you learned to hate my silence most,
but that is where I learned to see you,
most.

Interlude 37

it's always the goodbyes you never said
that haunts you most.

Waiting for the Light

I found myself drifting by the ocean this morning.
My faithful shadow only a step or two behind.

Surrendering the urgency in my ways
to her artless disposition,
I felt an immense sense of relief
as her warm sand rebuked the cold journey
from my feet.

I was ambling at the edge of my mind
when a familiar silence held me like lifetime lovers
at the commencement of eventual departure.

That is when you came back to me,
and the sea knew the anguish of ageless pain.

As the morning progressed,
I sat still upon my knees;
the sun-drenched sea rushing
like pallbearers beneath me,
waiting to usher away the parts of you
I had no desire to bury.

But I held you in the arms where reluctance
is no strange thing.
I pressed you up against my chest
and sniffed from your absence the aroma of love
and of longing.

I opened my lips,
but learned it is impossible to free the apology
that has grown accustomed to captivity.

And so, with silence in my mouth, I kissed yours.
And in the quiet space of the howling wind,
you bequeathed me a place to masticate your name
in this most beautiful valedictory composition.

And while my tears composed you,
I listened as the whispers of shallow waves
drowned out the thoughts of you that made it
burdensome to breathe.

Then you appeared as my reflection
snared my attention in the face
of the burning sand; a dimmed collective
of conversations that led nowhere
and kisses that held no agendas.

When I chose to release you,
I heard your voice in the ebbs and flows
of my sanity; coming and going as though
some distant thing had a feeble grip
on your attention.

And I listened.
For you see, the sea too, cries for you.

Navigating these uncultured emotions
has been the journey brave men take no pride
in speaking of.

Losing you has proven impossible to unlive.
And so, though you be nameless,
the lips that speak wonderfully of me
shall, too, speak wonderfully of you.

And though you be faceless,
the eyes that see something precious in me
shall, too, see something precious in you.

I still cannot see anything outside of you.
I still cannot feel anything outside of you.
I still cannot hear anything outside of you.
I still cannot taste anything outside of you.
And surely, I refuse to inhale anything
outside of you.

For you see, the existence of me has no place
outside the absence of you.

Interlude 38

i would ask you to stay,
but i'm not foolish enough
to think that a wildflower will pass on the chance
to dance with deciduous winds.

You Make Madness So Wonderful

You are a place void of noise,
and the chatter of my demons.

My mind is merely splinters of the thoughts
I keep of you, and yet thoughts I keep of you
are the only things that have proven
to keep me whole.

I am but the sum of the fragments
of your lies and indecisions,
but darling, you make madness so wonderful.

To kiss you is to vacate the ego,
and you have the most extraordinary way
of invoking the presence of God
between my wretched lips.

Hallelujah rolls so gracefully off my tongue
each time it savors the brown of your skin,
because darling, you make madness so wonderful.

And you remain—still—a native of my soul.
A captive of my hopes.
A fugitive before my tongue.
My darling, you make madness so wonderful.

So, perhaps someday, or better yet, some night,
at the culmination of this madness,
the December air and the quiet sea
will again be our witness.

Preferably bare feet,
and freed from the coverings of false pretense,
as I spend quality time inside your fleeting silence.

Our bodies covered in sheets of white sand
and snuggled beneath the cotton-like feel
of the moonless darkness.
O, my soul desires this.
Because, my darling, you make madness
so wonderful.

Interlude 39

yet another morning has found me
in the wake of a dream
that refuses to sleep.
and i love you,
unapologetically.

The Delicacy That You Call a Face

One day, I will appear out of nowhere;
much like the gentleman in the wind
that stole your attention,
sans permission.

You see, I saw the way you gave yourself to him,
carefree and committed,
sans reluctance.

I saw the way you held him;
permitted him to have his way with your skin
while transient freedom took advantage
of naked musings.

But as close as he's been,
he doesn't know his way around you
quite the way that I do.
He doesn't know the way you sigh
being kissed between the eyes,
and you don't know my only fear is that
there aren't enough days left to keep me honest.

So, one day,
I will appear out of nowhere,
and I will give myself to you to the falling away
of everything that doesn't adore you,
sans reluctance.

And I will kiss,
as though time is the fruit of my lips,
ever so softly,
and without a hurry,
the delicacy that you call a face.

Then one day,
I will go away,
but you will remain here,
picking up the pieces of yourself that you thought
meant something to someone else.

But when that day comes,
know that the ground takes nothing
from the worth of diamonds,
and know that diamonds have nothing
on the worth of you.

So, someday,
after this day,
I will come and I will plead for your attention
much like the gentleman in the wind.

And you will find yourself in my presence
the way you gave yourself to him,
sans reluctance.

And I will kiss,
as though time is the essence of my lips,
ever so softly,
and without a hurry,
the delicacy that you call a face.

Interlude 40

we found each other in winter,
right after the fall of summer.
we lost each other just the same.

Where the Heavens Kisses the Earth

I am the place where the heavens kisses the earth.
Where the disheartened sun lies in your eyes
the way lifetime lovers lie in the arms
of eventual goodbyes.

I am the place where the clouds ascend
like mountains; their spires adorned
a reddish fiery glow;
the consequential likeness of my heart's burning,
for you.

I am the lament filling the void of your presence.
The long night that has come so the day
shall no longer be.

Time and space here no longer honor
the vows we took,
but the way your wistful eyes glance away from me
when my crass ways conjure the sadness
of your deep, you have never looked more perfect.

Our light has succumbed to the darkness,
and I am again possessed by the sorrows I shed
those nights I clothed my heart inside the depths
of yours.

This is the day I have hidden my face from.
For though we conceived in the arms
of infinite possibility,

laboring through the afflictions of a broken love,
I must now bury this stillbirth of hope
that I once carried.

Eventually, the dreams I'll never wake from
will become poems I'll never write.
Wishes my tongue shall never speak.
The weeping of lullabies in the nights my body
holds tightly to the agony of losing you.

But until then,
I am the place where the heavens kisses the earth.
Where the disheartened sun lies
in the brown of your eyes
the way lifetime lovers lie in the arms
of eventual goodbyes.

Interlude 41

sometimes,
i deliberately sin
just to hear the way
her latin tongue
pronounces foreign blessings.

What Does It Matter Anyway

You may take me away, if you will.
A prisoner.
A straggler.
A companion.
What does it matter anyway?

Fear?
I'm afraid, she's not within your possession
to proffer.
But a moment to exhale the vestiges of familiarity;
what she feels like,
what she smells like,
what things of hers I shouldn't take with me,
please, permit me.

I relinquish my own strongholds.
Doubts.
Uncertainties.
Hope.
Desires to dictate destiny.

So, let her grass be tall, and her path be unpaved.
Lest I harvest where another has labored,
and know not the worth in the cultivation of pain.

You may take me away, if you will.
Your prisoner.
Your straggler.
Your companion.
What does it matter anyway?

Pretty Things Are Distracting That Way

Of all the thieves I've met,
none was more adept than time.
Yes, she inhabits a flower's nature,
but every touch serves as a reminder that in time
I'll wake up to nothing but a remnant of me
and not a scent of love left to make any sense
of you.

Your vacancy reveals things I couldn't see.
Scratches running up and down my
—loosely held—
sense of self as though some terrified part of me
has been trying to find its way out.

I suppose it means your presence
manifested my absence,
but pretty things are distracting that way.

The thing is, I don't know whether to curse time
for taking so much or thank her for leaving
so little.

You aren't here tonight.
So, brown rum has overrun the lies I placed
to contain this truth, and I admit,
I feel like a stranger to myself.

It is truly a sad way to spend one's birthday.
But pretty things are distracting that way.

Mastered Peace

Your art of death
brought so much life
to the canvas
of this prosaically mundane
existence.

Mist of a Prayer

I am here.
I am lying at my wit's end.
Merely the dregs left behind
after the last breath of faith dissipates
with the last prayer my fears managed to conjure.

I watched you, leaving, through the tears my eyes
couldn't hold onto any longer.
I simply had no vacancy for that much pain.

So, I left you there on the same floor
we lied on the night before;
laughing at nothing,
listening to each other's breathing,
and making the kind of love destined souls
find impossible to forget.

The morning after found us wrapped tightly
around each other.
Breaking fast, consuming one another,
but it could have been so much better
had you been there too.

God, I miss you.

You were tributaries of lovely words
dammed behind my lips,
and I was a trickle of incoherent expressions
escaping yours.

Somehow, raindrops always wrestled
outside our window.
Always fighting for a spot to watch
how beautifully love can blossom,
no matter how brutal the midday sun.

You were a whirlwind of unsheltered emotions.
The kind of storm that swallows whole
the faithless.

I was eager to navigate your frustrations,
but there were no commands of peace
found in my mouth.

So, you swallowed me up,
and I gave you up in the mist of a prayer
as I whispered you back into the ether.

Interlude 42

he was privileged enough
to talk you out of yourself
because you were foolish enough
to invite him inside the closet
God sat privately in with you.

Lie Down Beneath You

How does one siphon assurances
from empty promises?
I was your fool, wasn't I?
The fool warming his heart in the arctic wind
of words you never spoke.

How did I misunderstand time
calling you my forever
when you couldn't even commit
to the night that we spent together?

You relished the scent of my words.
Often, you'd wear them like some sort of fragrance
that made of feathers heavier souls.

You said they were like flowers
growing from my lips,
and you loved the way I landscaped your spirit.

Look how much I beautified you.
Crowned and molded you.
Now, all that I need is the shelter of you.
My colors fading beneath the merciless sun,
because you threw so much shade
when all I wanted was to lie down beneath you.

Interlude 43

here you are again.
crying.
drowning in those questions.
suffocating.
you carry that fear like the fruit of a woman
because selfish bastards like myself
are too quick to release the emptiness
that we carry on the inside.
this time the promises didn't leave my lips
before i buried them.
now, here you are, again.
crying.

Song and Dance

You are so blissfully ignorant
of the cracks in my perfect.

Just last night,
my lies stitched you back together.

That old song and dance you've come to find
so familiar.

But when the morning came,
and your monster went back into lurking,
you were there in my arms again
breaking at your mended places.

Interlude 44

i know the end of us is waiting outside that door.
i can hear it dancing to the wailing
of a broken violin.
i have no lies left to break your heart, my darling.
but the pain in your eyes has never
screamed any louder.
i know tomorrow's got no reservation for us,
but it's cold out, and tonight was kind enough
to prepare for us this shelter.
so, please, can we hold each other
just a little while longer?

All That I Am Is With You

The wind holds my attention so possessively,
and yet it passes with a distinct kindness
over my skin moving my being as though
I am rooted in nothing,
but still, all that I am is with you.

The ground beneath my feet is no stranger
to the burdens that weigh me down,
and yet it is never without strength
when I need it most,
but still, all that I am is with you.

Everything this world has to offer;
life,
death,
and all the irrelevances which lie in-between;
they are nothing compared to a moment stolen
from the noise, dancing with the silence of you.

So, give to me all that you are
while this night keeps the inevitable
outside that door.

Make love to me on this tear-soaked floor.
Because all that I am is with you.

Interlude 45

a late night and a sad song brought you back.
a forgotten memory washed ashore.
i am now in the deep,
the dark,
the forbidden place.
and as it turns out,
an empty bottle is no fit place
for the pieces of a broken man.

Let Go of You

My mind isn't free, available, nor unoccupied.
My situation knows many complications,
because it is rather complicated how
unsolicited evocations abuse intoxicated hearts.

You've become quite accustomed to the vacancy
that I carry.
I often see you in days I haven't yet lived,
and it scares me half to death knowing my skin
might become accustomed to your fingers again.

I find it so hard grasping this language called
missing you, though it lives daily on my tongue.
So, we miscommunicate often,
and that helps with the confusion.

Penning these poems from the pain
is like fetching water from abandoned wells.
They come most often at night when excessive
consumption of thought compels me to
regurgitate the pieces of you I haven't yet digested.

Do you know how hard it is navigating
your emotions when your heart only keeps
the good parts of the bad days?
Truth is, I would rather keep you where my
thoughts are breathless, but you always manage
to find your way between these pages.

Heavier days have led me to meditation,

focused breathing, mindful thinking,
but, darling, it is rather impossible to quiet you.
There isn't a single thought in my scope
of influence that isn't familiar with some facet
of you.
I've tried finding myself outside of you,
but each time I venture beyond thinking of you
I realize that I am not finished with loving you.

So, please don't you leave me to weather
these confessions all alone.
Tell me, again, I am your everything.
Kiss me again.
Call me darling.
Lay your wilting dreams before my lips,
and let me remind you how beautifully
wildflowers can blossom.

For you see, all that knows breathing
eventually knows not breathing.
And all that knows not breathing knows
the precious and precarious nature of time.

So, let us stop treating time like tomorrow
is already familiar to it.
Let's leave today with the pretenses we hide in,
so death will know what we look like
naked of the lies.
And before I too know not breathing,
allow my inhalations to be the excesses
of your exhalations.
Allow me to fill my vacancy with traces of you,
before I, too, let go of you.

Interlude 46

i watched tear stains marring that beautiful skin
the way ink stains marred the paper
i used to spell your name.
i've seen your struggle to find freedom.
i was there watching when fear took
the best parts of you.
i saw you hyperventilating
as though oxygen was scarcer than i'd been.
i saw you reciting zealous rebukes of the devil
who'd already made you, his possession.
you made depression so intriguing.
i saw that,
and i won't ever forget it.

Nightingale's Serenade

You've made a stranger your home.
So much vacant space,
still your dreams have no room to roam.

You dance, but alone.
You sing, but no one is there to listen.
So, pain and sadness cycle through you
like suns and moons through the illusion of time.

Your heart grieves you,
yet the flower upon your cheek withers from thirst.

You have forgotten the texture of love,
and, so, your hands upon my chest
interprets nothing but death.

And though the moon sits still in your window,
you are but the stone chosen by the Nightingale's
serenade.

Interlude 47

as for her lips…
well, they say the prettiest things

"hi"
"goodbye"
"kiss me"
"do you miss me?"
"i hate you"
"i love you, too"

You Stopped Showing Up

You despise me for choosing solitude.
I did not.
I chose us, but you stopped showing up.

I grew to love the dark, but it prostituted my
mind.
Funny how a touch of paint makes a cage
feel like a home.
My soul is bruised.
My thoughts are bloody.
Maybe love walks blindly because misplaced
loyalty always comes first.
Maybe losing you has been beating on me,
but who do you blame when you can't see
anyone but yourself?

It was my willing price.
My blemished sacrifice.
Gifting you what little I had,
and foolish enough to think that I was enough.
You looked so content outside my pain.
My tears spoke a language that was foreign to you
anyway.

You left me to time.
It broke me most times.
But I still found the time to spend time
with the absence of you.
I didn't choose this solitude.
I chose us, but you stopped showing up.

Interlude 48

the morning brought you back
in that ugly white dress,
black flip-flops,
and evidence the wind's been
in your head again.
you had the smell of regurgitated displeasures
and sun-burnt tears,
because expectations made you promises
they couldn't keep.
but i held you as if you never left.
i've used you so much i'll need a program
and a few years to get right.
but until then, i'll make good use
of this night.

Solus

I know solitude like no other man.
She's held me, comforted me,
provided me the room simply to be.

She's kissed me with every ounce of fervor
in her lips—spoken to me with the voice
of softness.
She's served me like a willing servant—seduced me
like a selfish lover.

At our commencing encounter,
I was as naked as the willow in northern winter
and completely covered in the evidence
of strangers' visits.

She touched me, and I wept.
But she knew a broken vase doesn't mean
the flower inside isn't perfect.
So, she spoke nightly, tenderly to my broken mess.

She arrayed me in words like precious raiment
and composed me in fourteen of the most
wonderful sonnets.
For it was fourteen nights that she held me
—provided me the room simply to be.

Time has since afforded me much company,
but it is solus alone that knows how to hold me.
It is her alone that knows the tongue I cry in.
It is her alone that knows the poems I lack

the courage to pen.

So, I am always in her company.
Alone.
A king.
A fool.
The joker that knows not the sound
of her laughter.
Away from the world.
From the noise.
Wrapped tightly in solitude's arms.
Because you're no longer in possession of the desire
to hold me back.

Interlude 49

familiar tears fell down her face
while loose garments fell to her feet.
she wanted so desperately to forget him,
but no one ever told her
open legs never bring closure.

No Greater Gift

I witnessed a flower blossoming
in a rainstorm.
She was dressed in a sentiment of unsullied love,
and wearing the colors of the sky that often lie
before the setting sun.

Overwhelmed by rain, by wind,
she was swaying like a woman in the arms
of burning desire.
I watched her, carefully, dancing slowly
with an amorous feeling
that was occupying my attention.

A gift she was.
A window into a world I'd only prayed for.

She unearthed a smile that was foreign to my eyes,
and conjured feelings that made me believe
I was worth something.

But then one-by-one,
she began gifting her petals to the ground
like the innocence of a lover weeping for love.
I felt a profound sense of sadness
gripping my heart as it were something
inside of me was afraid of letting go.
And though I saw her end, I was truly blessed.
Because she filled my cup from her emptiness.
And all that knows wisdom knows
there is no greater gift.

Interlude 50

your closed heart was no stranger
to my open mouth,
and for all the days i laundered my words
in bitter tears,
i was never able to wash away the stain of the lies
that soiled the purity of your trust.

Setting Suns Are Beautiful, Too

Interlude 51

for as the remedy in the bottle
does nothing for its breaking,
so the poetry in the poet
does nothing for his healing.

Brown of Your Eyes

Well darling, I am here again.
Eyes snared by a falling sun.
Searching the frames of memories
time hasn't stolen.
They only show your face now,
though the distance won't have me to picture you.

Sometimes the heart eclipses the mind
and the rasp in your voice floods
my quiet place again.

Sometimes, I take breaks from life,
buried beneath the lies,
and we both weep.

Sometimes, I come to you.
Sometimes, I undress you as though time
has no say in the way we abuse her.

Sometimes, I pull you in.
Sometimes, I hold you in the way I did back then.
Back when our bodies lied entwined in the same
place.
When we gave in to the comfort
of a worn-out couch while a sheet of darkness
blanked our nakedness.

Sometimes you'd say,
"Darling, I can't come any closer."
So, I'd inch my arms around you a little closer.

And I shed my walls the way I shed your clothes,
because between us, love needed no shelter.

Some nights, like this night,
I lie naked of you beneath the complete moon.
And I converse with the silence inhabiting
these pages.
Then I decorate them with unfinished poems
that we might have a reason to speak again.

This is how I know my soul isn't vacant of you.
So, I am here again,
wading in the hollow of myself.
Ebbing away in the inappropriate nature
of this solitude.
Clinging to contrived hope,
dusty yesterdays,
and uncertain tomorrows.

And though time is hemorrhaging faster
than I can stitch the wounds,
I am slowly orbiting that delicate sun,
dying in the brown of your eyes.

See, you were the fragile expressions on the lips
of a demented poet; as intimate as a lover's
surrender to purposeful touch.
But you always moved like the fleeting wind.
So, now the only evidence of your existence
are the fractures that prove, at least,
my heart's been lived in.

Darling, each time that a word departed my lips
with a sentiment of you attached to it,
death itself wept.
Breathing, you see, my air, was a clever excuse
to infuse my longing for God with traces of you.
Is this absence from you then not my ultimate sin?
And yet, is there a sin that can shackle the feet
of love?

Will you not seek me then, my love?
And when you find me,
will you not allow traces of God to infuse
my longing for you?

Darling, I know.
I know that I did not carry you well
in the brevity of my stay.
I know.
I know that I did not tell you that outside of you,
there was no song and harp to placate my demons.
I know.
I know that I did not love you wholly,
but I ask that you forgive me.
For I, myself, was only a fractured place.

My love, I have disburdened my soul
more times than I care to remember,
and breathless were the trees wherever my heart
bled in abundance,
but I have never written a word that did not find
its inception with you.

And that is all because I didn't give to you,

back then, everything.
Instead, I kept from you what you needed most.
That honest word.
The essence of a sentence I still serve
in the solitary confines of these torturous lines.

So many were the days—the nights—
that you begged me —hopelessly—
"Stay with me."
Your tears and your weakened eyes bearing witness.
But I was the romancer, you see.
The fool dancing with the silhouettes of evanescent
sentiments well beyond the permanence of you.

Foolishly, I was chasing the shadows of apparitions,
because the only place I ever knew life,
was lying in my darkness with you.

But I have finally fallen away from your grace.
This most monumental of my greatest tragedies.
And I am beginning to forget the little things.
The smile in your eyes when your heart let me in
—again—
first thing each morning.
The sound of your breathing when your sleep
is peaceful and deep.
The tenderness with which you held me
when my spirit was most weak.

I am beginning to forget the palpability
of salvation I felt in your arms as we lied
in the afterwards of the kind of love making
that compelled angels to fall for the daughters

of men.

All that I can feel now is the pain.
The pain that I so carefully cultivated
inside of you.
The despondent expressions of suppressed
emotions that you hid between your I'm OKs
and the tearful days.

There was, always, so much depth to your pain.
Such consummate works of art.
O, the curse of my tongue, and my indecision.

Darling, always, and subsequent to your
expressions of rooted frustrations,
your eyes knew the profundity of emptiness,
but selfishness compelled me,
rather than wiping them, to swim.
And so, I swam.
Far out and away from the shore that anchored
my wayward ways.

Tell me darling, how is it a man can be swathed
entirely in the macrocosm of love and never having
sacrificed such temporal ambitions?

I stood against you,
my love,
because pride promised he'd stand with me.
Now, look at me.
Naked,
afraid,
and so very lonely inside his company.

You see, darling, I betrayed your loyalty
engaging in acts of sin on the lips of a demon
that colonized my will.

Now, I have no place inside your garden.
So, I go about my way
—a vagabond—
bearing the mark of a foolish man.

But you should know,
I have relived the falling of us every second
of six-hundred and sixty-six days, a broken man;
rummaging through the vestiges of a delicate sun,
dying in the brown of your eyes.

And so, I frequent this place now.
Back here in the hollow of the emptiness
that you left me in.
A mere shadow standing on the outskirts
of the courage you mustered on your path
to rid yourself of me.
An apparition standing in the place of a man
seeking your permission to set himself free.

And I am still watching the falling
of that delicate sun.
Darling, I'm still dying in the brown of your eyes.

Interlude 52

your garden was home to the most
coveted moments.
in fact, i remember standing
inside your kitchen one gorgeous sunday morning.
the autumn clouds and timorous rain
had just passed on.
the flowers shimmered like diamonds
as the young sun admired his reflection
in the residue of raindrops
that the earth hadn't yet swallowed up.
i remember the taste
of your previous night
still clinging to my lips
as i sipped foreign coffee from the mug
with your name on it.
to linger in that space was to find
the most moving poems,
but that sunday morning
the strangest of things happened.
you see, i wasn't even finished
with the coffee that i was drinking,
but i walked away from your garden,
and all that i chose to remember
was the tiny crack that sat in the corner
of your window.

You Grow So Beautifully From Me

Soiled, but you grew so beautifully from me.
Moss green and flourishing.
You were floral patterns and divine mysteries
flowered with many suns.

I was there in your garden.
I held your soil in the benevolence of my hands;
caught wind of your essence each time the leaves
applauded your entrance.

So many moons have since risen,
so many suns fallen, but you linger still;
a wonderful fragrance upon my skin.

I was your king crowned with beauty,
with wisdom, and taking counsel of your silence.
But whilst I laid in your shade,
my arms were about the allure
of fleeting sentiments.
We became intimate until she knew my weakness.
But when I rose up from her,
it was your scent that lingered in my shame.

I allowed death to know the fertile nature
of your soil, my love.
Now, your birds no longer sing.
Your suns no longer rise.
Your stars no longer inhabit the vacant skies.
And I am soiled, but you grow so beautifully
from me.

Interlude 53

i’ve held you,
and i’ve not held you.
i am grateful for both.

Chasing Echoes

I am still haunted by the echoes of us.
In fact, whenever the house is quiet enough,
I can hear them bouncing between
the hollowed memories I keep us in.

As naked as late-night conversations
when impassioned hearts dare to get undressed,
they move like unrested spirits,
wandering through the emptiness
I never permitted you to occupy.

I still chase embers of the fire that we used to be.
They rise for stranger skies now.
Drifting away wherever the wind so wishes.
Faded, and fading.
They still displace the immediate darkness.

I long to lay my weary ways down next to yours.
To be consumed by that silent and persisted gaze
that always made a strange feeling of my strength.

You had a way of making me feel both lost
and not wanting to be found.
Such a wonderful state of confusion.
I long to wrap my heart around that feeling again.

Interlude 54

i still carry the scratches on my back
that enumerate the nights spent
between your thighs,
fasting from the lies,
while we patched up broken egos.

Do Right by You

The years they come, and they go, unlike you.
The darkness and its dismay keep finding their way
inside these poems I write, about you.
The solitude, that ancient enchanter,
he refuses to set me free, from you.

The ache in my chest persists.
The yearning in my soul is replenished each time
my mind digests some regurgitated memory
of you.

All this passion.
I conjure these poems like devout shamans,
but I still can't seem to manifest you.

Often in the mornings,
this empty house creaks at the places
your feet have been.
Sometimes I shadow your absence around
my familiarity, trying to fit these aging memories
around the perpetual novelty of missing you.

I swear these nascent feelings carry an older soul.
Because they take me to places we've cried together,
hurt together,
made love to each other,
broken each other.

I remember how your silhouette occupied
these naked walls.

Some nights, I pass my fingers over them
—leisurely—
the way I did you.

Sometimes, I scribble my confusion over them
—eagerly—
the way I did you.

And yet after all the writing,
after all the spelling,
I still can't seem to do right by you.

Interlude 55

i gave you the necessary room
to cry me out,
but if i'm lucky enough
that you should allow me back in,
i promise you,
i won't be the same fool
twice living.

Occupant

I am gone away, but I haven't left you.
I dance slowly and alone in my home
and even as the song surrenders to the silence
my arms are still around the vacancy of you.

I place my lips on faces
that cause not a feather
to begrudge my soul,
but at the sight of yours
the ground is not burdened at my presence.

I share my bed with a strange emptiness.
Some nights you stop by,
though you never stay long enough for me to see
how gently the morning opens your eyes.

But the fragrance of your voice
it perfumes my thoughts, still.
The serenity of your smile
it ensnares my words, still.
The anguish of your tears
it tears me apart, still.
And the scent of your soul
it tenants my soul, still.

Interlude 56

"why do you speak so beautifully of being hurt?"
i suppose being hurt is a cut in the heart
that reveals things we can't otherwise get to.
if that is the case,
i suppose someone or something must've
cut me quite deep to get such things out of me.
"but you don't speak beautifully to me anymore."
"i guess i don't cut you anymore."
it isn't that you don't cut me anymore,
i just don't have any more bleeding left to do.

Basin of Innocence

You were a place I was familiar with.
A home.
A belonging.
A sun rising from the residue of night's fall
and the moon's failure to hold the darkness.
My canvas of new beginnings,
you were the flower that bloomed from my ruin.

I remember a winter's night
and a candle's flame burning inside your eyes.
I remember my slim silhouette surrendering
to the calm you carried inside of them.

That night, I buried my cares
beneath your laughter,
for there was nothing left to mourn.

I remember tasting your smile behind a veil of rain
that kept the neighbors out.
You were three cords and a simple song,
but you made me do things my heart
could no longer prohibit.
A night more perfect than this has not reigned
over this world since.

Of course, time would be generous,
and I would speak reassuringly convincing you
to stand on promises I had not yet broken.
But time would move on, my darling,
and so would we.

And so, I spoke again.
O the witchery on the lips of a broken man.

Now I must bear these words,
my cross,
my burden.

My inclination to bare this aching soul before you
once again is the providence of love and of lovers.

So, I'll keep vandalizing my mind hoping
by these disheartened poems I'll someday
be healed of you.
You see, time away from you has not done
the one thing it was supposed to do.

So, I have become the picture of sleepless nights.
I am the sauntering day filled with reveries
I cannot realize.
But I submit to you this unblemished sacrifice.
These words born of a love that has not known
another lover.

Darling, the day will come when you will stand
to decree the sentence of my wrongs.
When it comes,
remember that love is the art of servants,
and I was fashioned for no lesser purpose.

Rest assured, I will not resist.
And should you need a place to cleanse your
hands, know that you will always have a place
in the basin of my innocence.

Interlude 57

how is it you took nothing when you left,
and yet here I am
filled with so much emptiness?

You Don't Go Away

Sunday mornings tend to bring you back,
but the midday sun is far more forgiving.
I listen as the quiet winds harmonize stiller waters.
It is a peace one can breathe amidst the chaos.
O but you, you are the bedlam that my soul
sleeps to.

You move so freely through the entanglements
of my situation; a wandering thought that asked
not my permission.
You have a tendency of stirring dormant poems;
wading through the silence that I use to hush you.
But I refuse to let you pool tears within my eyes.
For that is how I drown the demons inside.

You were the feel of aged leaves
and a timid breeze caressing the moments
that compelled my surrender.
A wayfaring poem composed of the ether
and sojourning within the walls I have not shared
with another.
Death was no contender for the way your lips
arrested my will, but now I'm indisposed
and running low on the breaths of you
that I take in.

Time has not been kind to the likes of me,
my darling.
But I hold you closer now than when colder nights
conveyed you to my bedroom.

Interlude 58

i never entertained a time so naked of you.
it is such a strange place to be.
a heart no longer free.
my shoulders comfort strangers
because my head never placed you
in the appropriate position.

i know the plague of resentful things
each time you pull me past my present.
you cease to weep when my illusions
have illusions of different outcomes.

so, the silence is haunting,
but i find respite in the shadows of night.
stronger drinks and sadder songs
making wrong things right.

i never made you happy enough
to forge a memory of that.
i have to live with that.
perhaps, i'll die with it, too.

Now That I Don't See You

Do you know the feeling of being wrong?
Deeply, profoundly wrong?
Has it ever sat you center stage when there was
no audience around to applaud your ego?
Has it ever kept you awake at night
while the world slept;
your mind tossing and turning,
fighting to escape the gravity of your decision
to choose you?

It has me, and I deserved every agonizing moment
spent in that prison.

Because you see, I was poison.
And I watched you slowly losing grip
as you slipped beneath the drip of words
that gradually chiseled away at the heart
my mouth was supposed to mend.

I watched how with each entrance of me
a bit more of you left the room.

I watched fear settling inside of you.
I saw how it clung to your eyes
before you closed them;
trying to hurry the pain back inside.

But you know, funny enough,
I didn't remember that tears sometimes
doubles as a mirror.

So, it was quite unsettling recognizing the monster
that occupied your eyes.

But you would grow, and time would have you
to become immune to my tongue.
And the scars became reminders of the chances
you afforded me to do right by you.

They speak of your becoming with such eloquence.
How strength found something worth saving
inside of you when weakness and I left you
to succumb to your wounds.

Playing victim,
I convinced myself that time would heal you,
my wounds.
But it has been so long.
So long, and all the medicine in the world
—it seems—
have conspired against me.

You see, time refuses to take from me the things
that I took from you.

You don't heal, my love.
Time doesn't heal.
At least, not the things we refuse to let go of.

And so, I ask, do you know the feeling
of being wrong?
Being deeply, profoundly wrong?

Do you know the feeling of being center stage
when there is no one around to applaud your ego?

The feeling of being awake at night
while the world sleeps;
your body tossing and turning as you fight
to escape the gravity of your own mind?

I do.
This is the prison from which I pen these poems
to you.
I want to tell you that I was wrong, my love.
I was deeply, profoundly wrong.

Sadly, I only see it now that I don't see you.

Interlude 59

and if you are really lucky,
you get to marry the fire
that freed your heart.

Hiding Place

A piano played a song for me today.
She said she'd lost the feeling of being free.
But then the present me found the absent song
between her missing keys.
And so, she played just for me.

It wasn't long before I realized that her playing
was my permission—permission to undress
her delicate song.
And so, my heart began unveiling things
fear could never conceal again.

O, she was beautiful, foreign,
and somewhat broken.
Still, I denuded her cadence
and we made flawless love
inside her flawless poem.

She didn't ask for much,
and I wasn't much.
So, it was only fitting that I gave her everything
that I was.
Key-by-key she opened doors I'd previously closed.
Note-by-note she poured out all that she was,
and I was just enough room to receive it.

You see, nothing's ever touched me quite the ways
she did as though something was unearthing
pieces of me I'd long ago buried.

As though my life and my death were occupying
a solitary moment.
And I was in no position to undo
what grace had done.

You see, her song caused flowers grow in the tears
she drew from a sadness I seldom knew.

So, we made use of an abandoned room
hidden within a wordless thought.
Then old memories rose up like stirred-up dust,
and our eyes began to cleanse our souls.

And while she played,
inhibitions fell to the floor our garments laid.
And we stood there in the cover of nakedness;
our fractured hearts dispelling bitter emptiness.
We were swaying like royal palms caught
in the charm of Caribbean winds;
her bridge providing me passage
against my desire to stay.

When the song was over,
she gave birth to a wonderful future.
And I became the present her memories
would never open.
But it would be everything listening to the song
between her missing keys again,
undressing her cadence,
and making flawless love inside her flawless poem.
It would be everything setting her free again.
It would be everything,
watching her growing from my tears again.

Interlude 60

like wandering footprints in dormant dust,
my soul still carries the tracks
of your vagrant tongue.
i've followed them.
they still lead to empty promises
and sinking feelings.

Late December

I stirred my thoughts like potions of deception
then bottled them in words of a similar fabric.
I knew your thirst, and they were rivers
of saccharine lies streaming along the banks
of my lips.

I knew your heart would break eventually
because you were that fragile thing my frail loyalty
couldn't commit to forever.
But I held you closely that night, Late December.
The first of the many nights you gave me
something I'll always remember.

Remember?
How your future felt like a present in my presence?
How your brilliant eyes made me break allegiance
with my darker self?
How I danced with your hopes
while you sat your fears aside?

You gave me your future that night
though all that I asked for was your number.
But as the weeks eclipsed the days,
and the months coalesced into years,
I became the deceiver you will always remember.

Isn't it funny, I claimed to adore your flower
all while drinking the water your roots needed
to see us grow?

I was watching you withering away,
and I was walking away.
But, you see, your roots weren't rooted in me,
and the tears I caused you to shed
your God turned them into your rain.

And so, each night, like this night,
as the clouds gather in weeping
and my mind lies immersed in a puddle of grief,
I make these attempts to write my wrongs,
but the very best that I can do are these
disheartened poems.

Darling, I've been trying to compose my way
out of this prison.
But still it remains, no matter how many times
I enumerate your name,
I know I'll never live to hold you, Late December,
again.

Interlude 61

i sat you down for a song i couldn't dance with.
my gut still hasn't gotten over it.
the muted moon and intrusive winds
often bring you back
whenever stronger liquor floods
the weaker parts of me.
O, but you never stay long enough
to see the way i sober up.

Counterfeit

It's been some time since I've been sober.
See, I've been spending empty nights
at the bottoms of empty bottles,
because I gave up eating you
for drinking toxic liquor.

Truth is, I've had my fill of missing you,
and I've grown sick of staggering through
these lonely nights.
But they are the only times I find balance;
the moments I find myself tripping over you.

I've been cycling through first date personas.
Searching strangers' eyes for something familiar.
Ah but you... you don't show up anymore.

All that I have left is a mouthful of empty words.
So, I've made a life of using pristine lies
to seduce weathered egos,
flattering broken strangers as often
as we dine together;
foolishly pretending older habits no longer
have a seat at the table.

Interlude 62

it is a delightful thing,
really,
watching a half-naked tree
getting fully undressed
at the earnest whispers
of persistent winds.

funny isn't it,
when the mind is empty,
the simplest of things embodies
the most breathtaking poetry.

The Way Pianos Do Violins

The sky weeps without.
Her grief percolates down the panes
of moss-covered windows.
Who would've thought voiceless raindrops
could express one's pain with such compassion?
The sound carries like the metronome
of a gorgeous poem.
I suppose I'm composing you, again.

The ocean exhales like a woman parting ways
with tremendous grief.
Her breeze salted, yet sweet.
It storms my lonely ways a welcomed disturbance.
I am taken away by the way it plays with my skin
while the trees surrender their leaves
to the invasion of evening.
I see you still know all the places my smiles
are hidden.

There is a sadness mounting my face
and a tear descending from it.
It is a secret my heart's being dying to divulge.
You see, fear lacks the capacity to possess lovers
destined for something, and thus death often
seduces his victims.
Sort of like the way pianos do violins.

This moment is as beautiful as it is heavy,
and I can feel my heart breaking beneath it,
but I embrace it like a lover I'd lost across a valley

of endless days.
I console it with the most tranquil of silence.
And I think of you, darling, the sole path
my feet wished never to end.

See, tomorrow has no place for a today
without regrets.
So, I pull you in slowly and with gratitude
the way wearied men do oxygen.
I hold you in tightly and with gratitude
the way mortal men do life when death
appropriates priceless memories.

"I love you" is a resident of my mind
though your room lies vacant.
And there isn't a day that do not speak of the
diligence that accompanied me
on my relentless search for you.
You see, I've been circling a straight path,
because I refuse to take a single step forward
without you.

I often think of your eyes;
the poems I saw your world through.
Someone else reads them now.
I pray they recite you with the passion I used to.

I still lose my way, my wits, and my words
in them.
I still hold you like a long-lost friend;
your face tucked tightly up under my chin.
I still dance with you slowly,
the way pianos do violins.

Interlude 63

i have become a necromancer of sorts.
i've been conversing with long gone things
buried beneath long gone feelings.
it doesn't frighten me
that i am afraid
to let you go,
and that...
that is what scares me most.

Either Way, the Pain Loses

I wish to be where I am not,
but I fear there is still room for me there.
I don't dare allow your name to flirt
with my lips anymore.
We both know my luck,
and God is humorous.

Whenever I begin to forget my way back,
I conjure you to the edge of my mind,
and there we dance in a circle of dreams
that are naked of this world.

You always appear dressed in sheer truth
trying to hide the lies,
and I wish nothing more than to fornicate
with every single one of them.

Every time I come,
I leave a residue of me inside of you,
and I kiss you with lips forged from inevitable
goodbyes.
Then I give you back to the darkness untouched.
Lest you step beyond the veil of dawn
and cause me to forget that the sun still shines.

I don't remember the way your body responded
when my fingers touched your soul.
The thing is, I am not sure if this is me healing
or if it is me dying.
But I guess, either way, the pain loses.

Interlude 64

remember how i broke my fasts
upon your skin?
how i took you in like sinful men
do communion come sunday morning?
remember how i drank,
sin intoxication,
during your moments of submission?
you were my church, darling.
my sermon.
my baptism.
my salvation.
remember?

Like Time Is Cyclical

Do suns still rise?
Do suns still set?
They rise and they set, still, for you, I bet.
I used to cycle, too.
Through rising and falling inside of you.

We were of the nature of night.
New moons' lights and astute winds
compelling slumbering trees to sing.
We were spilt passions and guarded poems,
intoxicated and open.

Your soft eyes and candid feelings.
My unmuted emotions, and bodily possessions.
The silence unveiling divine conversations.
Your face, my darling, was the only spell
I could not break.

Subjects of no laws written, or spoken,
we held time hostage whenever we held each other.
Your caramel complexion making of the darkness
a see-through dress.
My nude feelings revealing poems partially written,
yet as perfect as your silhouette.
My left arm wedged between your flesh
and a worn-out mattress.
My right hand creeping between the darkness
and your nakedness.

Because you see,
in a world of mindless conformity,
love is a rebellious stranger.
And so, I would feed on you
like I was fasting hunger.

We were residents of vacated insecurities
and unsettling uncertainties.
Cycles, without end.
Cowardice and confidence stripped bare
and making heavenly love
outside worldly inhibitions.

Darling, my respite was nonexistent until I drifted
into the shallow end of your breathing.
Divine healing.
Meditations and praises ascending from the fire
that we lit together.

We frequented each other outside the conditions
we found refuge in, and I held my breath
—always—
until you came.

Now, I'm merely a presence in your past.
Because though I've watched time open doors
to my flesh, my soul lies trapped.
Your legs still wrapped around my back,
I kiss you
like time too,
is cyclical.

Interlude 65

as if i have the room,
i break a bit more each time
i walk by a memory
you helped me make.

i've tried praying away the good days
hoping the bad would remind me
why today had no room for us both to be,
but i'm afraid god knows no such generosity.

Like Music

You used to speak to me like music.
Through music.
And though your tongue was foreign,
we never wrestled with misunderstanding.

Your lips had a way of anointing my shortcomings;
emancipation of caged feelings.
Darling, there was never a wrongdoing
in loving you.

Alone, out of my mind looking in,
and reflecting on recollections of you
has always been my favorite pastime.
The way we passed time.
You and I naked of prideful inhibitions
and touching each other's fragile perception of self
as though we were irreplaceable.

I remember when you rested my grief
against your breast as I wept like a pitch-perfect
piano being finessed by masterful fingers.

Your presence pulled such beautiful poetry
out of me.
Such beautiful alchemy.
Conversations of divine origins.
It was always an orgasmic encounter
watching your lips shaping air in the audience
of my ear.

I used to recite you like poetry that hadn't been
defiled by calloused lips.
But the last time we kissed,
you said you felt nothing.

Darling, I can no longer tell the difference between
loving you and complete madness.
Because I opened my mouth to speak your name,
but only uttered the ugliness that my heart used
pretty words to tidy up.

You used to speak to me like music,
and I've since been trying to explain to this world
that death isn't the soul living outside the flesh.
No, death is the soul living never having been
intimate with music.

You used to speak to me like music.
Through music.
And though your tongue was foreign,
we never wrestled with misunderstanding.

And so, when my life slow dances with my death,
and my God breathes itself into my dust again,
I will come again.
To dance.
To sing.
To listen.
To lose myself in your music, again.

Interlude 66

each time the elderly sun finds rest
and night falls like winged beings
seduced of sin,
i think of you, darling.
the sole darkness no measure of light
can rid me of.

Departure

His sun was setting with you.
Nothing quite captivating.
Nothing quite breathtaking.
Just his sun, setting with you.

Seagulls were composing peace aloft an angry sea.
Light giving way to darkness.
White sands being washed by water
that had seen the edge of the world.
The wind was expressive and free,
and yet no expressions of wonderment
found a place upon his captive face.

He lied naked with your lies
and conceived the bastard of his truth.
He cried inside your settled place,
but there was no healing
to wrap delicate arms
around him.

So, he left, at your feet, what remained
of the beautiful thing that had no eyes to behold it;
everything that he was;
everything that he wasn't.

His sun was setting with you.
Nothing quite captivating.
Nothing quite breathtaking.
Just his sun, setting with you.

Forgotten Place

The dust of our remains carries
a familiar fragrance.
It perfumes of pillow fights and raspy laughter;
unrequited anger and questions satiated by silence.

It carries us through the air the way sad songs
carry you through my glee.

I know it's time I swept these floors,
but nostalgia has a wonderful way of making
of a forgotten house a transitory home.
And even the transitory home is a coveted place
when the heart feels alone.

I have felt alone since the last time
you slammed the door to my face.
That night my heart shook to the jealousy
of the rattling windows.
It broke like the picture frame that slipped
from the grip of the living room wall.

You never came back to help me collect myself
from off the floor.
And from the looks of this dust,
it is safe to say that you never will.

Interlude 67

i am sitting beneath 11:25 a.m.
a complete moon adorning
the southwest end
of turquoise skies.

the sun is playing hide and seek
with winter's leaves.
my mind is searching wrinkled sheets
hoping to find some remnant of you
awaiting me.

i am thinking of the nights
my lips played between your thighs
while my tongue anointed your skin.
yes, we sinned.

i am thinking of your eyes;
how even partially closed,
they could show this complete moon
a thing or two.

All Seasons of You

This is all that remains now.
The place you no longer visit.
And time, here, has taken the form
of a frail old man.
He sits, always, naked;
the wrinkles of his mind immersed
in stagnant resentments.
Weightless.
Strengthless.
Hopeless.
Chains that keep him bound.

I live all seasons of you in a single day, every day.
There are neither sunrises, nor sunsets.
There are no moons to light the darkened skies.
The heavens birthed no stars here.
Darkness, my dear, is the color of everything.
My thoughts even.

The wind too has sat still since the day I left you,
and so, the trees have no one to dance with.

It's a strange thing seeing one's self
in inanimate objects.
But every place that I look,
I see some reflection of you gorgeously adorned
in some hue of yesterday.
Your happiness, tailored fit.
The smile you wear to express it still has no parallel
below the open sky.

You were the air passing through my aging lungs.
So, it is quite laborious, now, trying to inhale
your absence.

Sometimes, I cry to the heavens.
The whispered musings of your name wrapped
inside the empty parables I try to feed myself.
But my hunger persists,
and the ration of memories you left me with
are running low.

So, maybe in your world my ghost has found
its closure, but in this place, I am still seeking you
in a stranger's face.

Something tells me you've moved past me.
That I've been reduced to an occasional memory.
But you, my love, you remain my constant melody.
The silence I dance with to pacify my insanity.
The reason I'm perpetuating the misery
of seeing him loving you the way I used to do.

Maybe my madness has finally taken hold,
but something tells me that somewhere deep
inside your heart, inside your soul,
I still make you feel whole,
the way you do me.

So, this is my selfish plea.
My lamentation to the heavens that once
comforted our weeping hearts.

Proof of life.
Proof of love.
Proof that someday I'll see the way your face wears
the rising sun again.

I let you go, and I wasn't ready to.
I wasn't prepared for a time when I couldn't
watch you in the expression of your seasons.

Darling, I long for that feeling.
The feeling of your face buried in the comfort
beneath my chin.
Maybe one day this barren winter
will be kind enough to birth my spring.
But until then,
I remain the place you no longer visit.
Where all the seasons of you exist in a single day,
every single day.

Consensual

It was I,
like fire,
who burned out of control,
but were you not the oxygen
supplying my reason?

It was you,
like water,
who dowsed my flames,
but did I not keep you contained?

We Were

We were Sunday mornings unveiling
what Saturday nights hid between
our respective darkness.

We were wrinkled sheets
saturated in dishonesty;
a faint aroma of fracturing hearts.

We were spoon-fed nights while our flesh slept,
but our souls were not so confined.

It comes by no surprise then
that I seek you now that it is the end of me.
For we were lovers, and we were friends.
But we were beginnings waiting to end.

And so it is, darling, we were.

Fertile

In all the times I have seeded her fear,
she's only ever given birth to love.
Now, you tell me.
Is God not her refuge?

Interlude 68

you were a poem
waiting to be translated,
and i was a tongue
filled with misunderstanding.
so, i played often with your flesh,
but your soul was never amused.

Lingering Spirits

Sometimes dead things become lingering spirits.
There is an apology still perched on my lips,
and I denied you wings.
I am haunted by them both.

Daylight seldom reveals the demons possessing my
emotions, but the darkness is always so generous.

O, you were quite the artist.
Brutally honest, broken, beautiful.
The kind of liar that brings truth to tears.

Now and again, I get to witness your flawless abuse
of my mind.
I am usually just out of reach,
shackled someplace between your new person
and the pile of things you've forgotten.
You tend to withdraw yourself upon sensing
my intrusion.
But sometimes you linger,
and the sadness blossoms into midnight poems.

So, I pull you often from the darkness
and hold you between a residue of memories
we no longer inhabit.

Sometimes dead things become lingering spirits.
There's an apology that never left my lips,
and my name is absent between yours.
I am haunted by them both.

Interlude 69

i've lost enough of myself
to know that time is a slow erosion
of all the emptiness we've amassed over the years.
and though i don't have much faith left,
i pray sometimes,
though with much deficiency of hope,
that the one thing it will leave me with
is the sight of your eyes consuming my person
in those moments you felt i was actually
worth something.
i was my most beautiful self inside of them,
even if i was only an illusion.

Best Poem

Within the heart and its apportioned time,
love is the sole constant in the time
apportioned me in this heart occupied by you.

Self-encounter, what a beautiful tragedy you are.
Contentment has known so few the breaths
I let out or took in since the day you exhaled me.

Excavate what remains of me,
and I'll reveal all the places I have buried you.
Self-encounter, what a beautiful tragedy you are.

The empty heart knows many roads,
but you are the cul-de-sac that takes me places.
Dreams often find me adrift in delusions of us,
for it is only the darkness that permits me
to see you now.

My tongue, often, finds ways to penetrate you,
but the questions you conceive
often come forth still.

I ingested you before our time,
but such clarity you were to my aged soul.

Don't you see,
you were my freedom,
my prison,
and my inspiration.
Darling, you were my best poem.

Interlude 70

i used to be the place you'd run to
when the place you'd rather be
didn't have the room to accommodate you.
But i suppose you've gotten tired of the running.

The Someone Else I Should Have Been

Somewhere, some place this night,
someone else is slowly undressing
your conversation.
They are lying naked with the secrets
I made you cover up;
holding you a little closer
than this loneliness does me.

Somewhere, some place this night,
someone else is knowing you the way I used to do.
Piece-by-piece they are stripping you bare,
and I am here falling to your feet
the way soiled garments do.

So, in this night,
and in all the darkness that is yet to come,
I will sift through the pile of things
I never said to you;
holding to a dated version of me
while the present you lies enraptured
by strange eyes,
strange hands,
and prettier words on a stranger's tongue.

Tonight, strange lips are speaking life into you
the way I didn't do.
In wisdom, they are placing you on the pedestal
that I stood on as I watched you fall.

I know that I did you wrong,
but you're acting as though it wasn't my bed
that kept your dreams off the floor.
As though it wasn't my arms that gave you shelter
when you grew weary of their monster.
As though it wasn't my lips that sipped the tears
you shed because of them.

Tell me, old friend,
would the rising sun know the elation
of the morning had the darkness not come?

You share your fire with another
as though it wasn't I who fanned your flames;
as though it wasn't I who supplied them oxygen;
as though it wasn't I who made you know
the feeling of consuming something.

You withdrew our past from your memory bank
as though our time wasn't freely spent.
But I'll always keep an account of you.
And I'll always use this pen to check in on you.
You see, I didn't plan to write this night,
but evidently, I'm still holding to a few pieces
of you.

Come morning, you will set me free
until the shackles of night fetters my hands again.
Then it's back to a weeping heart and a restless pen.
A broken and a lonely man writing envious things
about the someone else I should have been.

Interlude 71

the mind you once lived in
is now your coffin.
the crying in the night has become songs
i sing to set you, finally, free.
the pretty words cut fresh from my soul
will die before long,
and time,
like dust,
will take the best of you
and the rest of me.

you were the honest truth cutting deep,
but i bandaged the wounds with sterile lies.
so, there's a remnant of you left in my scars;
pathways to the worst parts of better days.

i don't have the room to accommodate you
tonight.
i'd kiss you goodbye,
but i've gotten tired of the lies.

Of the Nature of Love

I remember when your words felt warm.
Safe.
How they danced like untamed flames
and the way I disrobed my soul
of resident disquietude before them.

I remember when they became cold.
Toxic.
How I wrapped my ears around them
and held them inside like a wounded friend.

But then your words became distant.
Silent.
Still with my entire heart, I listened.
And not to my surprise, love was still there.
Speaking.

You see, though you grew dormant,
love was still moving.
And though I lost my way
when I found my place inside of you,
love was still there,
guiding me back to myself.

Interlude 72

the first night that we met,
she ordered white wine and i spent the time
envying the way a long-stemmed glass
sat between earth-toned lips.
we talked until intoxicated honesty
began leaving our hearts unchecked.
then she stripped away her flesh,
and i saw for the first time
the last thing i'll ever forget.

That Hour Again

I am dying in the presence
of a guitar's serenading
sentimental longings,
You are the subject in each of them.

It's become too familiar standing alone
beneath this cold shower.
The scorching water cascading
down my naked skin,
and I can't feel a goddamn thing.

Don't you see it, darling?
It's that hour again.
The window that lets the demons in.

Interlude 73

the first morning that a night gifted us,
i witnessed you breathing me in
like the aroma of a meaningful praise.
in the end,
you were but the transcription
of my fractured existence.
but o, what a wonderful sentiment you were.
my heart's spillage
beyond the confines of my lips,
you be.

Beautiful Reason

While the morning aged
and hope struggled for a breath of reason,
I followed the footsteps of fading familiarities,
pleading before a council of lucid dreams.
And you, my beautiful reason,
were the wisdom emanating from each of them.
A tranquil fountain of placid emotions
suspending my breathing.
I became as death;
lifeless,
entirely sundered from you.

I glanced down and my feet were submerged;
paralyzed in a murky puddle of persisted pain
that distorted the fabrication I thought myself
to be.

I caught sight of my shadow moving to the paced
and captivating wailing of a wistful violin.
Illusions of better days teasing with illusions of us,
and feeling this Autumn wind against my skin
is akin to the way your insistent fingers
wrested compassion from repressed sentiments.

This morning you appeared as shades of freedom
—radiant—
and dancing with the silhouettes of palm fronds
arrested by the easterly wind.

A manifestation of the rainbow God drew
from my ruin.
A reminder that I will never again be this broken.

Yellows.
I still smile at the very thought of you.
Blues.
I wonder, do I still remain with you?
Reds.
I'm losing myself, again.
Black.
I went beyond, but you weren't among them.

No one there possessed a tongue
to render me helpless.
No one there possessed a face worthy
of my numbered days.
No one there embodied the healing
my mouth often extracted
from the brown of your skin.

So, now I'll have my needed rest.
Because death, my beautiful reason,
is so very selfish.

Interlude 74

lead me bare feet to the path unpaved.
bury me a memoir
where the willow seduces the wind.
please, open my wings.
allow freedom to have its way with my fear,
and i will love you to no end.
dance for me when you know i'm not watching.
kiss your very best memory of me
as though i never left.

Time in Displacement

The months and their days gather between us.
The minutes and their seconds unfold time
like the nuanced pitches and tones that birthed
barren words inside your fruitful mouth.

I cry, at times, because tears tend to ease the burn.
It is my foolish way of holding on to losing you.
But each time that old sun goes down
for one more sip of the ocean's kindness,
time takes one more piece of you,
and peace from me.
I am always in two places, you see.
The place we met, and the place you left us.
They still manage to pool the pain inside my eyes
no matter how much I pretend you aren't with me
anymore.

Even now,
I am here in the arms a black night holds me with
—o such profound emptiness—
and it hurts so much knowing, come morning,
someone else will witness the way your eyes
eclipse a rising sun.
They will know the secrets they keep,
and the reasons I chose to lose myself in them.

But you're fading.
You are fading.
So, I guess the silence has finally gotten
the best of you, old friend.

Interlude 75

and when the light retreated before the night,
i sat in attendance of your absent voice.
i was hoping.
wishing.
praying.
watching old tears carving new paths
down my aging face.

Of the Nature of Living

Attempting to seduce death,
I, sometimes, speak from loose lip.
O but that is the way of the boy
I never set free.

I tend to torture these pages, come night.
Can't say I know why.

I get beside myself,
scribbling answers to questions I never asked.
I really should burn them when I get done,
but I'd probably just end up hanging around
to inhale the ash.

I guess a mind plagued with pain is one way
of denying death glory.
But must you really exist in every which way
I express what little of me I have left?

I just sat to witness a breathtaking sunset.
Next to me a daffodil dancing at the edge
of the darkness.
Tell me, is there anything left that you won't
mock me with?

From the Ash

I held you in my hands.
Like fire.
Watching as you slowly consumed
those parts of me death had already bartered for.

I began to weep.
Not of denial.
Not of anger.
Not of bargaining.
Not of abjection.
Not of acceptance.

No, I wept for the sole purpose
of dousing your flame.
And I doused your flame.
And no flower has since risen from the ash.

Interlude 76

i have given my hands to countless women.
my time,
recycled lines,
and the shallow end of my mind.
but my deepest regrets,
my saddest sentiments,
and the poems that occupy the softer side
of my hardened heart,
they will remain with you.
they will—always—remain with you.

Pieces I Am

Misplaced, these pieces I am.
Still, through the shallows of the shadows
we once called home, my soul continues to roam.

With regrets, I regress to warmer nights.
Our naked aspirations flirting
with midnight passions.
I can feel your arms wrapped around my neck.
Your face is buried inside my chest.
There's a generous violinist here
and she's guiding our unhurried steps.
I'm timing your exhalations to breathe you in.
Not even God, my darling,
has ever been this close to me.

Sometimes, I attempt to surface
for a breath of freedom beyond us,
but the memories pooled inside lies vast,
and profoundly deep.

Sometimes, I drift while I sleep.
Sometimes we meet, bare feet,
somewhere between your need to be away from me
and my need to tell you that home still feels
like me.

I remember that time a night's morning
saw us together.
You and your bare feet were on the way back
to leaving me desolate.

The rising sun was unveiling things
the crescent moon kept hidden.
My anxious heart was sinking beneath
the tranquility that took residence in your eyes.
Your lips were repelling the silence.
"You feel like home again," you sang.
So, I pulled you in,
and I held you closer than you've ever been.

When I awakened, the sheets perfumed of you.
I could still narrate the texture of your skin,
translate the pattern of your nervous breathing,
and o, the taste of your lips lingered sweetly
—still—
inside my mouth.

Since then, subjugating my soul to the pen,
I have written countless poems,
but I haven't managed to get you out.

My heart often speaks when it thinks
no one's listening.
Things no arrangement of words
are worthy to undress.
You wouldn't fathom how deeply it still carries you.

I know, my words were few when I had you.
In fact,
"I am tired of sitting in this silence with you,"
you often said.

But silence, my darling,
was the farthest thing away from me.
You see, whenever I was with you,
my spirit babbled like a nervous fool
losing touch with his composure.
But somehow, my lips couldn't afford the words
to clothe the naked feelings that were native
to my loving you.

So, I gave ears to your frustrations,
but no comfort was found in my mouth.

Eventually, I surrendered the privilege
of holding you for empty eyes
and even emptier conversations.
But perhaps the silence in this book
will speak loudly enough,
and you will hear clearly enough,
how deeply you still move me.

How deeply you still stir me.
How deeply you still hold me.
These misplaced pieces that I am.

Interlude 77

"do you love her?"
cautiously.
"why cautiously?"
because i was fearless once,
and you are the scars to prove it.

Naked and Not Ashamed

Everyone needs a friend.
Someone they can open up and run freely in,
naked and not ashamed.

I am by no means perfect.
There isn't a day that lives and dies
that does not remind me of this.
See, the moon bares herself in a company of stars
—naked, except for her scars—
and still, she is a master at snaring the eyes.

No matter how many times
I've bared myself inside of them,
there was never a hint of judgment
in the expanse of your eyes.

My fears.
My scars.
My polished truths.
My naked lies.
With you, I carried no walls to hide behind,
and yet, I was always so safe inside of you.
Always so whole, no matter the pile of my pieces
that lied at your feet.

These days, I pass time inside eyes
that do not know I exist.
I search them in search of you.
But imagine endeavoring to birth love
after having been intimate with fear.

I am diseased again, old friend.
Inflicted by the tangible presence of your absence.
This hellish deficiency of your company
induces ailments, and the remedies lie only
in the flower that knows the air of your presence.

You see, old friend,
you were always that book I could open up
and run freely in,
naked and not ashamed.

So, I pray we'll meet again like unrepentant fools
and sinful habits.
That I'll be burdened and you completely open.
Because, you see, old friend,
I need, once again,
to run freely inside of you,
naked and not ashamed.

Always Here

The pages of my journal lie bare,
and yet, I have no desire to be intimate with them.
Lord knows,
I have given birth to numerous poems,
because I couldn't miscarry you.

I, sometimes,
see you in the falling petals of Fall's flowers,
and I am the aging Summer's grass
waiting to receive them.
Insanity, you see my darling,
has been more gracious than you'd been.

But the distance is dissolving now.
The warmth of your lips walking across my face
while the low-lying moon repelled the darkness
ahead of them, it has come to visit me once again.

The wind often takes us wherever it wills,
and every place leaves me breathless in your eyes.

I composed you, once, in the residue of passion
that blanketed a sunroof window.
It was the night we permitted love to know love
in the privacy of our naked words
and partially veiled bodies.

I can still see the fallen sun that persisted
in your eyes that night.

I can still feel it's gentle rays caressing
my unclothed soul.

Some nights, I still sip of the poison.
Those toxic words that gave us reason to question
what destined souls ought not to.

I often rise in the arms
of the same dreadful morning,
hoping she'd washed me free of you.

But you are still here.
You are always here.

Interlude 78

a nervous feeling fills my throat.
a word arrested in fear.
i sense you are somewhere near.
somewhere,
hiding in the shallow of my soul.

Room

This room carries you, so well.
It carries everything about me
that your absence didn't take.

The morning that led you away,
and the night that never brought you back.

It carries echoes of the fear that inhabited my lips
when Love was pleading to be heard.

It carries that song.
The one we used to lie with,
listening to the darkness,
outside of words,
but within arm's distance of a Spanish Guitar
and her intimate dance with a soothing violin.

It moves through me still,
through this room,
the emptiness I've become,
as though there are no other here.

Interlude 79

i'll always envy the spot in the sand
where your butt cheeks sat.

Strange Place

I am a strange enough place,
though I carry a familiar sentiment.

I have always been infatuated with the sight
of the journeyed sun sitting low in the burning sky.
The way it nestles itself above the place
where the gentle heavens lay loving lips
upon the delicate earth.

We sat here once, you and me.
You told me, "Darling, don't you dare allow
that charming sun to kiss me in places
your lips are foreign."

And so, of empty words,
I fashioned you a promise,
but, today, I regret to say that I never lived up to it.
It was for this reason that I wrote you that poem
in the ocean's sand,
right below the place you laid loving lips
upon a traitor like me.

I wrote it with every bit of diligence that occupied
me, albeit only to watch as a herd of waves
carried you off into the waiting deep.

Then I watched and watched until the heavens
were dressed in all black.
Until the ocean mourned her fallen sun.
Until the air was pungent with regret

and the tears I held on to
as I watched you walking away.

Then I allowed you
to overrun my chance to love me,
the way an angry sea reaches land
it wasn't meant to be.

I know I don't deserve the tears you shed
in those memories I find impossible to bury.
But when the heavens were dressed in all black,
and when the ocean mourned her fallen sun,
I sat there, and you appeared out of nowhere,
but well within the proximity of my insanity.

And I felt my soul breaking free
as you laid loving lips upon a delicate me.
And I loved you then as I love you now,
with all that is left of me.

I broke you so much you had nothing left
to leave me with, a parting gift.

So, I am a strange enough place now,
though I carry a familiar sentiment
somewhere inside here.

Interlude 80

i knew the fire in her arms,
—quite well—
but the rain falling from her eyes
soothed me too many nights
to notice the burn.

Visitations

My heart doesn't have the room.
So, we often commune beneath the open sky.

I go inside and all the voices sound like you.
All what I feel feels like my lips falling
like morning's dew atop your cocoa skin.

You no longer grace my mornings,
but my nights still welcome your visitations.
So, go ahead, my darling.
Possess them as only you can.

For there is no holy water.
No holy scripture.
No zealous preacher.

I have fallen,
and nothing can redeem me now.

Interlude 81

far as i know,
we only get one life.
one try,
then we die
whether or not we actually lived.
but if it be that god sees fit sending me back.
i'll go back to that same spot.
order that same drink,
take that same sip,
rest my elbows on top that same sticky counter,
and wait again for our commencing encounter.

The in-Between

I am here between Friday's night
and the familiar light of Saturday's morning;
somewhere between guarded fears
and the deflowering of my inhibitions.

I am strung out on memories of you,
and lying face-down in regurgitated pieces
of the same.

I am thinking of your eyes
and the resident softness that occupied them;
how they often emitted sentiments of setting suns
just before tranquil oceans begin to swallow them.

They always led me back to you,
but your tears have since muddied the path.

And though Saturdays' mornings
are no longer familiar with us,
some Fridays' nights I lie down with you,
watching how tenderly your touch unveils my soul,
though there is much work to be done
in the manifesting of my shadows.

You were always so beautiful clothed
in the parts of my mind the darkness
has yet arrested.

Interlude 82

this is the place i fell for you.
right here!
it was right here that i first tasted you.
this is the place a generous moon
revealed your face.
the place i first felt like i could
and would fight giants,
to be your chosen space.

this is the place i found you.
this is the place i cried for you.
this is the place i buried you.
and it is the only place that will never
allow me to walk away
no matter how many cut flowers
i've watched rot with the apologies
you refuse to accept.
right here!

Here, You Remain Still

Last night, I left some space between my arms
and enough room on my pillow to accommodate
a memory of you.

But when the sun came,
and the light drove the last bit of hope
from my eyes,
I realized your spot was not slept in.

I rose up, with much reluctance,
from the pain that I slept in;
the rising sun incrementing the days
that are gathering between us;
your name moving between my tongue
and my silence.
For this is how I pray now.

I have learned time eventually aborts the things
we don't give birth to.
But I will part ways with time,
before I part ways with you.

So, I dream you, still.
I envision you, still.
I carry you, still.
In spite of him.

Did you know, I sensed your existence
before a name became so privileged
as to set a mark of distinction upon you?

But I wear this body like a coffin, now.
I sleep in the arms of dying things,
dreaming of the life I knew with you.
I am wandering about the absence of you
guided by your waning laughter.

For when my heart knew vacancy,
I conjured you into my own possession,
and there is no water,
no vain repetition,
no prayer that possesses the power to expel you.

I will never exhale you.
I will never speak your name
to the transience of time.
I will never permit a thought to clothe my mind
if it be naked of you.

I love you with an enduring love.
I love you with an enduring love.
I love you with an enduring love.

And here, you remain still.

A Little Time Less

Why does death rejoice over us?
Has he not been around long enough
to know that I come back for you
at the dawn of every life?

You may go, my life.
Be one with everything that lies contrary to me.
Let the childish wind show you what it means
to be free.

For when I come again,
I will undress your essence
with a tongue full of patience.

I will see you more.
I will touch you more.
And I will heal you more,
a little time less.

Interlude 83

the moon sits perfectly
in the raven sky
and like nothing else.
yes, i was your deepest darkness,
but i held you perfectly
and like no one else.

Stranger Now

I fell from you like a tree's casting of dying leaves,
but your feet were my position of praise.

I saw the detour in your eyes
the last time I made you cry,
but what is love if not potholed roads
and shortcuts leading back home?

So, I showed up,
bruised up,
with a mouthful of empty words
that left your deflated heart gasping for air.

But I feel like the stranger now.

I've had my fill of empty conversations
over well provisioned tables,
but I crave your silence still.

I am lying still.
Trying still.
Telling you the prettiest things;
like the mysteries of the heavens
and the parallels I found only in your eyes.

I became invisible the night they stopped looking
my direction.
I watched the pain getting deeper with time
until it swallowed me whole.

So, I cry, sometimes, from here,
because you left me an unfamiliar place.

And I feel like the stranger now.

The open sky knows the frequency
of the pain that I pray in.
It used to bring you back to me most often
while night made its transition to morning.
But it seems some other darkness
has since garnered your attention.

So, I feel like the stranger now.

Wait for Me (Espérame)

Beyond the nights love was never made.
When raindrops danced atop worn-out roof tops
while lightening lit pathways to the bed
I wasn't welcomed in.

Espérame.

Beyond birthdays not celebrated,
and the words that spilled from anger-filled lips
because uncultured passion consumed
the very best of us.

Espérame.

Beyond that warm couch that kept
our coldest secrets;
where your naked truths
dispelled my shrouded lies;
your legs serpentined around my thighs
while I emptied my silence inside your eyes.

Por favor, Espérame
(Please, wait for me)

Interlude 84

the trees are here baring themselves
before the wind again.
it reminds me of the way
i used to remove excess clothes
from your gorgeous skin.
slowly, and with so much grace.

Walls

I remember the days when these walls
protected you.
Now, they are splinters of disappointments.
Merely fragile residuals of a forgotten sanctuary.
Frail and painfully honest,
they speak always of regrets.

I left you open for the shelter of another someone.
Now, you are another's someone.
And resentment, that old doddering demon,
he keeps teetering at the edge of my mind,
refusing time's petition to make good use of him.

I am as broken as the home memories
are no longer made.
I sound like emptiness.
I feel just the same.

I remember the days when these walls
protected you.
Now, they are splinters of disappointments.
Mere residuals of the sanctuary
you found your prison in.

Interlude 85

and always remember, darling,
let your mind be the crown of thorns
that protects that flower you call a heart.

Trespasser

You search my lips the way sound searches silence.
You pass your fingers over them
as though my heart speaks in braille,
but you have yet to accept your blindness.

This thirst for words that you possess
is enough to leave my throat dry.

Trying desperately to find your strength
inside my eyes, you've birthed a reverence
inside of me for the diligence inside of you,
though it is a thing of fables, my darling,
fetching water from stricken stones.

I've watched you speaking with your body
like a mute channeling words their lips
weren't familiar with.
The way your eyes canvassed my face
while tears depleted your soul,
I was entirely speechless.

And as you sought your freedom,
fighting to express the things
I never permitted you to speak,
I choked at the cracks in your voice
as they swallowed up the message
you were trying to send.

Such a despairing disposition.
I saw you then,

how beautiful you were when you weren't whole.
So, I selfishly gathered your broken pieces
while you were trying to collect yourself.

For what it is worth,
I wanted so badly to ache for you;
to cry for and with you,
but behind these eyes,
I was as empty as the silence you conversed with.

See, there is nothing here for you, my dear.
The words you seek to hear,
the reassurance that's been prolonging
the eventual breaking of your mind,
I have long given to someone else.

But should I yield to the innocence time and age
hasn't deflowered me of, you, my dear,
are worth so much more than any lie
these lips could ever try to sell you.

So, don't you fall for me any further,
because the hands that should catch you
are holding someone else.

Don't you shed another single tear,
because the lips that should kiss it away
are kissing someone else.

And don't you look at me again,
the way you look at me now,
for what you see now
has long belonged to someone else.

Interlude 86

i could have held you forever.
o, but you never did understand
the measure of a moment.

Faded Footsteps

These floors entomb the remains of you.
The house, too, is cold, mostly quiet.
'Cept, tonight, my mind is soaked in cheap wine
and intoxicated with priceless reveries of you.

Truth is, I've been praying for a happy medium;
trying to correspond with the ghost
of your presence.

It hasn't been easy living off cold tears
and sad songs,
but it's been this way since the day
I began fasting from you.

This is how I listen to you now.
How I leave myself behind whenever I get
to missing you.

You should know, I've wept.
Swept up what was left of your faded footsteps.
And as cold as they are,
these floors too speak warmly of you.

This is how I listen to you now.
How I replay the sound of your walking away
for the very last time.

Interlude 87

“how did it feel?”
“when i left, how did it feel?”
it felt like the universe was crying with me.
“why do you say that?”
because it was raining that day,
and rainy days are the worst days
to ever leave someone.
“i’m sorry.”
yeah, me too.

Interlude 88

i will miss this.
i will miss our conversations.
our listening to music.
our silence.
i will miss this.
i will miss the fights that led us to peace.
the peace that led us to love.
the love that led us to us.
i will miss this.

The Portrait of Time

A shadow's leaf holds gently to the wind.
A slow dance to a piano serenading
pleasant reminiscence.
A portrait of time succumbing to gross negligence.

And this...
This is a silence of sorts
I'd spend the balance of my soul to listen to.

A bluebird hides the daylight's brooding.
A blackbird's somber recitation in the twilight.
A half-moon seldom tells the full story.

And my sun has fallen from the edge of your eyes.

A host of teardrops croons in the gloom.
A weeping heard from afar.
A solace enshrouds the chaos
of a day's collapsing in my arms.

But at least I held you 'til death was through.

A generous breeze has brought you by.
A wounded memory left far behind.
A violin eulogizing departing feelings.
A prayer rising from the pages I burned
to breathe you in.

Don't you see, you are here, my darling.
We have reached our end, and you are still here.

something pretty?

your eyes.

A writer, thinker, poet, and mentor, **C.L. Brown** was born and raised on the island of Jamaica. He immigrated to the United States at age eleven. As conveyed in his work, Brown is profoundly inspired by the very essence of life. His work has garnered him much acclaim for his poetic style and accent-rich delivery. In the words of American Actress, Kimberly Elise, Brown is "changing the world one brilliant and authentic poetic word at a time."

He's authored several poetry collections including ***Bare, and Loud Whispers of Silent Souls***. Residing in Miami, Brown enjoys gardening and spending time with his life partner and daughters, Luna Marverly and Sunday Sky.

CPSIA information can be obtained
at www.ICGtesting.com
Printed in the USA
LVHW101056160622
721218LV00041B/619/J

9 781735 031101